DISPERSED CITY OF THE

PLAINS

DISPERSED CITY OF THE
PLAINS

HARRIS STONE

with JOAN STONE and J. WILLIAM CARSWELL

MONTHLY REVIEW PRESS   MR   NEW YORK

Library of Congress Cataloging-in-Publication Data

Stone, Harris. 1934–1995
     Dispersed city of the Plains / Harris Stone.
        p. cm.
     ISBN 085345-992-4 (cloth). — ISBN 085345-993-2 (paper)
     1. Architecture — Environmental aspects — Great Plains.
2. Architecture and society — Great Plains.   I. Title.
NA2542.35.S85 1997   9726930
720′.47′0978dc21   CIP

Monthly Review Press
122 West 27th Street
New York, NY 10001

Manufactured in the United States of America

10 9 8 7 6 5 4 3 2 1

CONTENTS

FOREWORD

When Harris Stone learned that he had cancer and a limited time to continue his work, chapters one and two of *Dispersed City of the Plains* had been completed, but only a typed text existed for chapters three and four. He set to work immediately on handwriting and illustrating the remaining text and reached page nineteen of chapter four, before he could no more than lay the groundwork for others to complete the book. I took on the handwriting for the final pages, and J. William Carswell, a colleague in architecture at the University of Kansas, took on the drawings. He decided to make them distinctly different than Harris's: dots instead of lines, pencil scanned on the computer instead of pen and ink, all the same size, not very large, and set off from the text. Barry Newton, another colleague in architecture, agreed to write the introduction to the book. He and Harris argued out many of the ideas as they worked together on historic preservation projects in Italy and the plains region.

In a letter to the editor of Monthly Review Press, shortly before he died, Harris summarized his thoughts on *Dispersed City of the Plains*:

> Fortunately, before this medical problem came to a head, I had a significant breakthrough in my struggle to penetrate the built forms of this region, which has enabled me to perceive the unique structure of the American city and its implications internationally. The poet Thomas McGrath was right when he observed, "North Dakota is the world." . . . The four chapters of this book present the basic argument about the dispersed city of the plains and my hypothesis concerning the built form of the American city, the built form of monopoly capital. My intention was to write an additional chapter that explored the implications of this hypothesis here and abroad (especially in Italy), but the argument is complete without it. Who knows? Others might be inspired by the argument and wish to test the hypothesis themselves.

Most important to Harris and what he would want to be remembered for are his four books, published by Monthly Review Press, which he saw as a single, evolving work-book: *Workbook of an Unsuccessful Architect* (1973), *Monuments and Main Streets* (1983), *Hands-on, Hands-off* (1991), and *Dispersed City of the Plains*. They are illuminated manuscripts of our time, a record in text and and image of his indomitable, critical, enthusiastic, and imaginative search to penetrate what people have built and what it means.

Joan Stone
Lawrence, Kansas

ACKNOWLEDGMENTS

Matthew Newton and Wendy Weiss for their photographs of the plains region; Dennis Domer, Associate Dean, School of Architecture and Urban Design, University of Kansas, for reading and commenting on the text at various stages of its development; and Cynthia Muckey, Director of the Computer Resource Center, School of Architecture and Urban Design, for her help with computer and copying tasks.

INTRODUCTION

Much has been written in the past few years about architecture and regionalism. The conclusions vary, but the idea of region as existing beyond the realm of climate and topography is universal. The general assumption is that the region as institution must be made obvious, and that only then, when a deliberate and mythic representation is known, can worthwhile activities take root. For this larger view to carry authority, the circumstances must be clearly examined, and for that to occur, the present realities must be faced straight on, unobscured by transferred typologies.

This book explores the form and consequences of the inhabitation of the large landscape of the plains, a landscape where the demarcation of property preceded settlement. As such, the making of form is based almost exclusively on the play of economic forces, settled directly and without sentiment or a prior attachment to place. This world of property, which is recognized as being unique within its early forms of settlement, is by now, 150 years later, almost ubiquitous at a national and possibly global scale. The narrative therefore examines the attempts to create place and value within this proprietorial grid. It suggests that improvement will not occur in these forms of property until older notions of settlement have been left behind.

The method of argument, commentary, and demonstration, as in the three previous books by Harris Stone, depends on the powerful dialectical possibilities of texts and drawings. Each offers a potent tool for completing arguments, while creating space for the interpretations supplied by the individual reader. The sources range from the vernacular (quotes from a quilter) to Foucault's complex archaeology of knowledge, and within these contrasts the authorial position emerges, both sympathetic to the human realities described and detached as an intellectual construction.

The settlement of the plains began with the functional elements associated with the agricultural practice: enclosure, storage and the acquisition of suitable power sources (Chapter 1). These entities—fence, silo, and windmill, without which permanent and productive occupation of the land would be impossible—are then left in the landscape, and the necessary progress of dwellings is examined as the settlements succeed or fail (Chapter 2). The beginnings of economic and social order establish necessary densities within the grid; hamlets grow into towns and cities, or remain as vestigial representations of the previous occupants (Chapter 3). The model of concentration and dispersal, of engulfing waves of pestilence, storms, and drought, change the landscape until, in the final section, the cities and their regions begin to detach themselves from a solely agricultural function, and are patterned instead around the changes in regional and local transportation and communication (Chapter 4). They become representations of a transnational, global economy.

Throughout this chronology of inhabitation, *Dispersed City of the Plains* examines the relationship of individuals and families against the background of natural and political forces. In all of the stages described, the desire for community, education, and control guide in the making of a concrete phenomenological world. This world is interpreted as a commentary upon and contest with the implacable but developing background.

Two major ideas are formally advanced. First, the movements caused by the economics of land cannot simply lead to the creation of dense enclaves in or around the city. The romantic propositions of human settlement advanced by Steven Holl and many others seem to suggest that architecture can promote community rather than respond to it, and are similar, although not exactly a mirror image, of the naive idealization of the grain silo as form encouraged by Le Corbusier. The text shows that the latter's view was far from the lived reality of grain production and trade. The second idea that can be developed after the romance is gone is the capacity and need to adapt the prevailing methods of building construction to the making of the place. The author insists that we do not abandon the possibilities of industrial production in pursuit of human satisfaction. The 2 x 4's of the balloon frame made possible the inhabitation of the treeless plains, and here the question is posed: could making more advanced techniques of construction available lead to the possibility of a more self-fulfilling architecture? Clearly this question will not be answered if land as property is reinforced by the commodification of architecture, in which modern constructional techniques lead to a thin and mistaken assemblage of motifs.

This book also demonstrates a tough-minded examination by an American of an epitomized landscape of America. As a companion to the three previous books, the present text recognizes the contributions of craft and idea. The optimism that emerges in the final section, which looks at the world of malls and suburbs, can only be explained by the discovery that, in and around the apparently bland form of the late twentieth century city, a persistent contest and resistance is present. A spirit of human affection, association and making, is set against the incomprehensible largeness and forcefulness of corporate capitalism, in ways that are similar to those of the earlier occupants who moved into, and made a life within, the sparse and inhospitable plains. This is a guarded optimism, however, that looks to an analysis of the city and its region not founded on Pienza or Montepulciano, nor on the order of proto-European settlements like New Haven, but on the unfolding patterns of the plains themselves.

The forces of dispersal that now predominate must therefore be seen as a starting point for an analysis of future possibilities. This book shows in a focused way that the European idea of the central city neither corresponds to the reality of the past 150 years on the plains, nor recognizes the more fluid methods of communication and publicness that seem daily to extend our lives. The capacity to resist these new circumstances is, once again, the adaptation of the pre-existing grid, with its implications of ownership and methods of production.

Beyond the persistent themes of the grid, the climate, and an ever-changing economy, Harris recognizes the power of work. This is the work of settlement, and the work of building and renewal. The concluding chapter suggests the necessary work involved in having the courage to abandon the old myths of townmaking. Faced with the reality of dispersal, it promotes the critical work of making lives and ideas within the settings of proprietorial anonymity. One of the required actions is the remaking of abandoned structures; the second, the remaking of ideas.

The work on the Barber Schoolhouse (Chapter 2) continued alongside the writing of this book. This building grew out of a strong, even passionate commitment, and has gone through periods from vitality to senescence, then neglect.

A building that was made in 1871 by great communal effort against a backdrop of marginal settlement and a desperate agriculture, when immigrants invested their lives into community through education, is rescued in 1996 by similar forms of engagement. In the waning years of the twentieth century, the context is remarkably different, and these differences, combined with the persistence of the structure, inform and establish the architectural program. Architecture now precedes property.

The new roof owes as much to Charles Eames as local forms and profiles. It hovers above the stone walls, supported on eight slim steel columns, forming three internal bays with thin trusses clad in corrugated galvanized steel. The new floor pays its debt to Carlo Scarpa. The local limestone scraps from a contract to clad a corporate high rise are laid as regular cut sheets. Although it may be argued that these efforts with one building are only of interest as a demonstration, it is precisely the idea of demonstration, of edification through the edifice, that propels this and the previous actions and works of Harris Stone. The capacity for intellectual enquiry and thoughtful physical work allows the fabric of the structure to re-educate a new generation, to replace a neglected structure and reposition the associated landscape, both actually and intellectually—one building and one book at a time.

Barry Newton
Lawrence, Kansas

GRAIN ELEVATOR,

BARBED WIRE FENCE,

WINDMILL

...she stood far off on the bank of the river. And she said, 'For what do I go to this far land which no one has ever reached?'

And Reason... said to her, 'Silence! What do you hear?'

And she listened intently, and she said, 'I hear a sound of feet, a thousand times ten thousand... and they beat this way!'

Reason said, 'They are the feet of those that shall follow you. Lead on! Make a track to the water's edge!... Have you seen the locusts how they cross a stream? First one comes down to the water-edge, and it is swept away, and then another comes and then another... and at last with their bodies piled up a bridge is built and the rest pass over.'

Olive Schreiner

PREFACE. Built forms of the Plains are approached in this essay in such a way that an observer can draw a set of basic images from the cultural landscape.

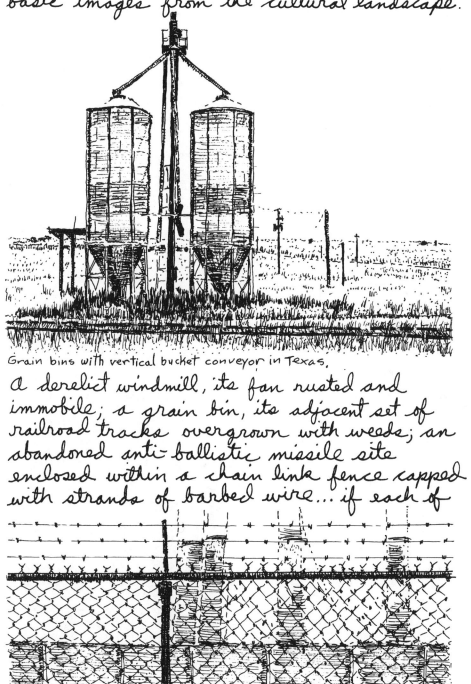

Grain bins with vertical bucket conveyor in Texas.

A derelict windmill, its fan rusted and immobile; a grain bin, its adjacent set of railroad tracks overgrown with weeds; an abandoned anti-ballistic missile site enclosed within a chain link fence capped with strands of barbed wire... if each of

3

PREFACE

these images is viewed as a reaction to a problem, as an attempted solution, the outline of a series of questions begins to emerge. This questioning gaze at particular situations can penetrate the surface of things, their stylistic labels, and focus on the common experiences, the building practices and trends that give shape to built forms and are, in turn, modified by them.

These experiences occur, these trends manifest themselves according to different time frames, in response to different events, and with different effects. New architectural problems and attempted solutions are superimposed on those inherited from the past. One built form accommodates the process of adaptation and change more readily or forcefully than another. In the 1920s Le Corbusier was inspired by images of grain elevators; fifty years later, in a situation called an "energy crisis," the attention of designers shifted to the image of the windmill. Today

PREFACE

the image of barbed wire is a symbol here in the great Plains -- and elsewhere. Its significance as built form has emerged out of a cumulative pattern of activity: the brutal, unrelenting activity of constructing this fenced-around cultural landscape.

Union Stockyards in Chicago.

What is striking and interesting about these built forms are the social relations which people have established among themselves in the course of transforming the landscape and the consequent transformation of the symbolic capability of their activity.

PART I: GRAIN ELEVATOR

After a diagram by Le Corbusier in *Towards a New Architecture*.

PRIMARY FORMS ARE BEAUTIFUL FORMS.

Anyone familiar with the literature that heralded the development of modern architecture is aware of this famous "reminder" to architects and the accompanying photographs of grain elevators "the magnificent First Fruits of a new age," in Le Corbusier's book, Vers Une Architecture (1923). Today the photographs have an ominous quality and might be captioned, "the Only Fruits of an industrialized countryside." Such a reaction stems from an awareness of the violent destruction occurring outside the frame of the cropped images, the violent destruction of nature.

Calumet River.

In the built form of cylindrical grain elevators and cubic support structures the repression of nature presents itself immediately and starkly to the post-modern observer, who cries out, "ugly, just plain ugly."

However, in Le Corbusier's "new age" of mechanized building procedures, as in any age, built forms are neither beautiful nor ugly per se. What is more, all that is ugly in the industrialized countryside can be rethought,

6

reworked, even removed by an architecture that identifies the ugly as such. The history of architecture is comprised of new versions of old building types, "good" design supplanting work that is condemned as "terrible." The rural landscape, no less than the urban center, is a sequence of building efforts, each correcting "mistakes" of the past.

The particular form of grain storage in Le Corbusier's book represents one moment in the history of a building type that dates back to the earliest human settlements and plays a constantly redefined role in a constantly redefined struggle for survival. The function, grain storage, has not varied, but the form has -- from culture to culture, age to age. It has developed and changed in response to conditions that have developed and changed, producing regional variations similar to dialects of a verbal language. As in any language,

Dogon granary built beneath sheltering rock overhang.

Grain silo from Yenegandougou.

the surface features of these regional variations have been shaped by powerful cultural undercurrents. The photographic images may be viewed as "primary forms," not in the sense of cylinders and cubes as Le Corbusier suggests, but rather in the sense of their inner historicity.

This inner historicity, this collective undercurrent repeatedly cracks through the function and generates variations and modifications of the built form. For the intents and purposes of architecture, the collective essence of grain storage is enshrined in this sequence, and this apparently subjective imagery is collective in kind. The antagonism between image and function reproduces itself generation after generation. Le Corbusier's image of grain elevators was shared by an entire generation of architectural students, practitioners, and commentators. Bernard Rudofsky's image of "semi-sacral" granaries in the popular exhibition and book, Architecture Without Architects, played a similar role in helping the following generation dismiss Le Corbusier's "reminder" and articulate different ideas about the relationship between

8

the natural and built environment, between machine-built structures and those built by hand. Nevertheless, within the body of work produced by each generation and each building system the attentive observer will find one particular example of grain storage ugly, another beautiful.

Grain elevator at a bend of the road.

The question remains: what is the significance of this kind of reaction to such blatantly utilitarian built form? There are related issues similar to the well-known debates about photography or "primitive art"; and they should not need another go-around: Can a grain elevator be considered as architecture in the same way or to the same degree as a cathedral or palace? Yes. Is the use of it as an architectural image separate from its original function valid? Yes, but... at the time that

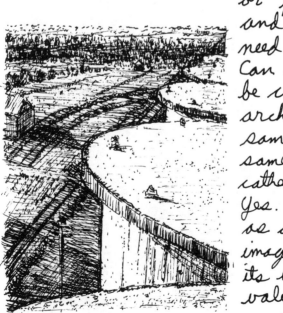

Elevator roofscape.

9

Le Corbusier was discussing the grain elevator
in terms of its geometry,
wheat was being cut
with a binder or header,
threshed in a separator,
hauled by wagon or
truck, dumped into a
pit from which it was
hoisted by a steam-driven bucket chain into
the storage bins that caught Le Corbusier's
attention, and eventually piped into railway
boxcars -- surely not a sequence of "primary
forms." Forty years later, at the time that
Rudofsky was
presenting granaries
as images of the
divine, the bulk of
grain produced in
the great Plains
region of the United
States was being
sent to port cities
and loaded onto ships
with overseas
destinations. From
the outside the
grain elevator
might still be seen
as a row of concrete
cylinders, but inside
it was an interlocked
system of vertical
and horizontal trans-
fers controlled from

Grain binder in operation, 1920s.

Grain elevator loading a barge.

Elevator interior at ground level. The bins are supported above an open floor; swivel chutes discharge grain into pits from which it is hoisted to the headworks for redistribution, a console that blended the grains and directed the mixture along belts that extended as much as a quarter of a mile to a waiting ship— an animated sequence, even if it did not add up to Rudofsky's description of granaries as having the appearance of "dancing." Despite their conflicting notions about architecture, both Le Corbusier and Rudofsky created images of the beautiful by ignoring unattractive facts, not the least being the fact that the storage of grain represents the only resource more central to the modern world economic system than the storage of oil. Ugly reality, as antithesis of beautiful images, continually gnawed away their utopian affirmations, which eventually disappeared in a haze of architectural nostalgia.

Architecture can not be equated with the beautiful nor abolish the ugly. Ugliness, no

11

Stern (left), Eisenman (right)

matter what it may be in a particular context, is an aspect of architecture, actually or potentially. For example, a "deconstructed" tower designed by Peter Eisenman is the beautiful purified of its ugly counterpart, a process which a "classical" designer, such as Robert Stern, speaking in the name of the beautiful, pronounces ugly.

In literature containing information about the grain elevator the word "agriculture" tends to mean more and appear more frequently than "agribusiness," but the latter tends to signify the operative force. The

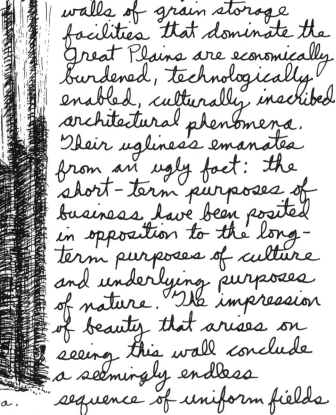

Elevators in Oklahoma.

walls of grain storage facilities that dominate the Great Plains are economically burdened, technologically enabled, culturally inscribed architectural phenomena. Their ugliness emanates from an ugly fact: the short-term purposes of business have been posited in opposition to the long-term purposes of culture and underlying purposes of nature. The impression of beauty that arises on seeing this wall conclude a seemingly endless sequence of uniform fields withering under a relentless sun coincides with an appreciation of the mathematics of the situation. In this regard Le Corbusier's perception of it as geometry is appropriate, but paradoxical. Something else can be seen

Port of Chicago.

in his photographs besides the geometry of the grain elevators: roads, rail lines, waterways — that is, the movement of grain. Further, beneath this system of linkages lie older ones.

Town of the Plains.

This part of the country is subject to irregular rainfall, a year of flooding followed by years of drought. For the buffalo and the Plains Indians who pursued them, to travel vast distances was essential and, given the regularity of the landscape, manageable. Their homeland was not a compact area, rather it was a web of meandering lines. This gossamer system was obliterated in the process of marking out a few new lines: the trails on which people moved westward and, later, cattle northwards. The underlying pattern remained, however, and was reinforced; life in the region is still largely dependent on moving through it.

The elevator is a point on one of the more recent lines to be inscribed on the landscape and culture of the region: the movement of grain from field to factory. Getting wheat from here to over there depends on the infrastructure of trucking, rail connections, and shipping suggested in the retouched photographs in Le Corbusier's book, which, however, obscure its details through an artful manipulation of the images. The foreground of one photograph is a texture of four parallel lines converging towards a vanishing point, lying on a continuous grid of ties and suggesting an attractive, if unrealistic railroad yard devoid of trains.

Loading a railcar.

After an image by Le Corbusier.

14

"Railcars are never available when we need them," a commentator angrily observed, "and when we do get them, the rates favor the big grain companies." He later muttered, "the railroads are abandoning the little used spurs to small elevators... a thousand miles of rails annually are allowed to grow weeds."

The foreground of another of Le Corbusier's photographs is a flat plane that seems to be a paved area large enough to accommodate trucks. Another suggests an immaculate waterfront with a passenger ship steaming into the middle ground.

Railcar loading shed.

After an image by Le Corbusier.

"A traffic tie-up may interrupt the flow of wheat by truck," writes an authority on the grain trade; "an untimely freeze on the

15

Harbor canal.

Mississippi River can interrupt barge traffic; a mechanical breakdown in a port city, a dock strike, a storm at sea can affect the movement of wheat internationally."

The problem of glorifying the domination of geometric shapes over landscape and culture was that Le Corbusier's formalistic modernism diminished the actual scene that inspired his abstract compositions. However, in trying to define the content of the ugly and beautiful in this context, his impassioned argument and manipulated images should not be dismissed, for they dramatize a situation and indicate that, as built form, a wall of grain storage facilities is something more than a cut-and-dried description of what it does.

"Grain elevators are located in most every farm community," another author observes, "and often compete with the local church steeple as the highest

16

Grain elevator in Kansas.

structure around." He finds it appropriate that a poet referred to them as "Sentinals of the Prairie." These capitalized words constitute the spirit of the built form for poet and the historian who fondly recalls them. "Sentinals of the Prairie" defines grain elevator not merely as blind appearance, but also as appearing essence. This verbal distinction, in turn, is closely related to various philosophical formulations and, as such, may sound unrelated to this or that aspect of storing and moving grain. However, grain storage facilities are not only objects built in particular places to function under particular circumstances, they also constitute a building type endowed with a spirit -- acknowledged by Le Corbusier, Rudofsky, poet, historian, most people moving through the Great Plains. This spirit transforms the particular object from being merely a thing among other things into something animated, something that can reach out as it is approached, something that can touch people's lives.

17

"When I dropped in on the North Dakota town of Rolla, farmers still had a lot of unsold grain from the recent harvest in their bins, and they were gambling all the time," a commentator on the grain trade recalled. "Several in-town elevators buy grain in Rolla, but they offer almost identical prices. These were changing rapidly, even crazily, in response to fluctuations in Chicago, and wheat growers were poking their heads in all day long to stay informed... It was agricultural roulette..." And like the form of roulette played with a loaded gun, this game was deadly serious. After a brief pause, the

commentator added, "the farmers who were still in business in North Dakota plainly liked the excitement."

A visitor may have found the scene enacted at the Rolla grain elevators attractive at the time, but the underlying situation was and continues to be ugly for most of the wheat growers involved.

The spirit that animates the elevators is not merely the storing and selling of grain, which is embodied in and symbolized by their built form. Nor is it the general outline of the structures, which Le Corbusier described as

"primary" built forms. It is more like a source of light, which illuminates the scene enacted that day in Rolla, and it emanates from a configuration of qualities: the siting of the grain storage facilities; their massing, building materials, and construction details; how they are used and linked to one another; how they have changed over time.

PART 2: WIRE FENCE

BEFORE THE MID-1870s the great Plains was open range country; by the end of the decade it was not. Countless tales, ballads, films -- even scholarly studies have transformed this brief episode into an element in that popular myth about "the way the West was won," in which barbed wire is suddenly and inescapably attached to the land, cutting modern America from a simpler, more natural way of life that existed "once upon a time."

When the first fences were made, the cattle, never having had experience with it, would run full tilt right into it, and many of them got badly hurt. Some man would come into the range, where the stock had regular rounds or beaten ways, and fence up several hundred acres right across the range... After the first three

20

years of wire fences, I have seen horses
and cattle that you could hardly drive between
two posts, and if there was a line of
posts running across the Prairie, I have
seen a bunch of range horses follow the
line out to the end and then turn.

from Cowboy Life in Texas

All the versions of the story agree on
two basic facts: farming requires fencing and
fencing in the barren Great Plains had
appeared to be an insoluble problem.
Elsewhere in the country fencing was
accomplished primarily with wood,
secondarily with stone and thorny plants,
but here there was no timber, little
stone, and thorny trees, such as osage
orange and mesquite, were slow growing --
if they grew at all. During the critical
period, 1875-80, discussion of the problem
occupied more space in the printed matter
produced in the region than any other
single issue. People were casting about
trying, inventing every sort of fence
imaginable.

21

Remains of hedge fence in Kansas.

Barbed wire; without the Industrial Revolution it would not have been possible; without the Great Plains it probably would not have been necessary. In other words, the invention should not be isolated from its historical context: the continuous process of territorial expansion, the development of the railroad and of the homestead acts, the killing and repression that play such a dominant role in the mythology of the "Western" adventure story. The story of the fence is interlaced with profit making, bad conscience, and deceit; it is the objectified spirit of manipulation and control of land and culture. In the 1850s agricultural expansion had ground to a halt. It was barbed wire that made it possible for agriculture to resume its march across the Plains; it enabled farming of blood stock cattle as well as crops to replace

22

ranching as the dominant occupation of the region. The fence asserted itself in economic calculations, legal prohibitions, technical criteria -- that is, the whole specific weight of nascent agribusiness.

A poet recalled the struggles of his parents on a farm in Nebraska in a book printed in 1917 titled, Barbed Wire and Other Poems. The title poem begins with an image of "the prairie cleft by skirmish lines of fences," and then relates various forms of skirmishing:

... Gray's front foot
is doubled in size, stiff, lumpy, hairless too.
The poor colt pawed that hoof over the fence,
And pulled and sawed for hours. The pine tar
With which we filled the wound did heal it up.
Horses are horses. Curses on barbed wire!

When longhorns overran the settler's land
The herd law would not grant him damages
Unless his crop was fenced. Hail to barbed wire!
...

Writing towards the end of the century, Thomas McGrath perceived the essential continuity of these skirmish lines in his poem, The Fence Around the H-Bomb Plant, which concludes:

As your palms, from touching the wire,
    come away red:
Think: your own argument is simpler
    if you can state it--
If you can read the lines that rust
    in your hand
Or unravel the reason of this
    fenced-around world.

It is possible to unravel bits and pieces of what McGrath refers to as "the iron logic of the fence" in the ghost towns of the region, for a rusty stretch of fence may be the only built form marking the spot, the only indication of a struggle lost or one threatening to erupt.

Pitcher, Oklahoma: the center of the largest area of zinc mining in the world between 1915 and 1930. The busiest corner in town was the intersection of Main and Second Streets; the liveliest area extended about three blocks along Main, a block to either side. By the end of World War II most of the zinc had been mined and government subsidies stopped. By the early 1950s the once lively heart of downtown was a fenced-off wasteland of

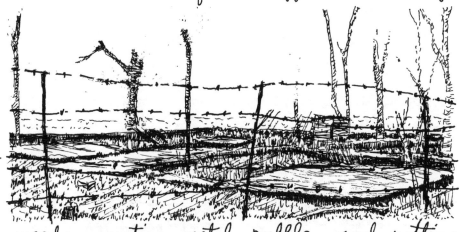

weeds, rusting metal, rubble, and rotting wood. In less than 50 years the entire town had been dangerously undermined, most dangerously in the central area, which in a matter of a few months had been vacated, razed, and sealed off with barbed wire.

Dahlen, North Dakota: in missile silo country, 1987. Surrounding the site is an eight-foot high chain-link fence, topped with the obligatory three strands of barbed wire; on each side a sign is posted:

WARNING

RESTRICTED AREA
IT IS UNLAWFUL TO ENTER THIS AREA WITHOUT
PERMISSION OF THE INSTALLATION COMMANDER
(SEC. 21, INTERNAL SECURITY ACT 1950, USC 79)
WHILE ON THIS INSTALLATION ALL PERSONNEL
AND THE PROPERTY UNDER THEIR CONTROL
ARE SUBJECT TO SEARCH.
USE OF DEADLY FORCE AUTHORIZED.

A man and a woman walk around the fenced
enclosure peering through the wire mesh
at the humming thing inside, leaving
footprints in the melting snow and mud.
The adjacent town is little more than
overgrown railroad tracks, a grain elevator,
a few houses, and a row of shops with
boarded-up or broken windows, left open
and empty.

Nekoma, North Dakota: an abandoned
anti-ballistic missile site. A four-sided
pyramid looms above the prairie. The doors
have been removed, but the three-foot-thick
concrete and steel walls remain and rooms
with bunks and shelves. A message was
once scribbled on a wall -- then painted
over -- only a few words are still
discernible "... a 272 million dollar..." A
fenced compound of carefully boarded-up

26

houses and warehouses the size of a small town stands nearby.

The wire fence delimits the landscape and culture of the great Plains and crowds out what does not fit: first, the buffalo and the life of the Plains Indian; then, longhorn cattle and the cowboy; then the ventures that haunt its ghost towns; currently, small scale agriculture and the family farm. "This fence, this barbed wire is most assuredly ugly," an indignant observer concludes. Another sees it differently, "There may be something dangerous about it, something that lacks refinement, but there is something else as well, something harmonious with the relentless hardness of the Plains." The fence has its own law of form: its purposefulness, and it is beautiful to the extent that it adheres to its law of

form as a matter of fact.
The "Introduction" to
the book, Land of the
Post Rock, begins with
this observation:

Ordinarily fence posts would not be considered
scenic attractions. But such distinction... belongs to
the creamy, brown stone posts that grace the
landscape in north-central Kansas. There, where
woodlands are sparse and prairies expansive,
[farmers]--however inadvertently-- complemented
the natural scene by setting out rows of stately
posts, all shaped from the native rock now
known as Fencepost limestone, or simply post rock.

Viewed from a technical vantage
point, the object and the inner
dynamic of its parts appear
to the authors to well up from
the land itself. The "Introduction"
continues:

The aim of the early settlers
who started the practice was
not to adorn the landscape

Wire/stone detail.

28

but rather to fence their property. To do that, they were obliged to find a substitute for post timber, which was not available... By chance or by necessity, they began turning back the sod and splitting posts from the rock layer that subsequently was named for its use. By coincidence the finished posts were colorful and when set in place along the fence line blended with the landscape.

The book examines the climate, geography, and geology of the region; the need for and development of barbed wire; the tools, methods, and procedures utilized in quarrying, manufacturing, and installing the posts and attaching the wire.

No matter how technical the contents may be, the book concludes with a chapter titled "Majestic and Durable They Still Stand," and an impassioned plea: To preserve the post-rock landscape is an obligation the people of the area have to the state, to themselves, and to all the visitors who come to admire it. In short, the authors argue that a set of conditions at a particular place and time produced a technical object -- barbed wire stretched between stone posts, which they perceive as possessing the beauty of the landscape into which it was inserted -- by necessity, not aesthetic choice. They argue that such beauty can, indeed must be preserved and suggest how:

... In 1956 a motel, restaurant, service station complex was dedicated under the name 'Post Rock Motel'... Since [then] 'post rock' signs have become legion throughout the area. The term has been incorporated in names... in slogans... in promotional brochures and on labels for souvenirs.

The validity of dismissing this notion of preservation as a trivialization, or worse, a kind of vandalism of regional history, might seem self-evident. However, the disparity between "post rock" printed with quotation marks to indicate its use as a trademark and without them to signify a building material echoes a disparity between the fence as something built and as something observed. It also

echoes a disparity in the fence itself -- that is, between stone post/barbed wire.

If the notion of preserving the "post rock heritage" is to have any validity, it must include not only the post rock, which may appear to possess beauty, but also the barbed wire, whose ugliness can not be smoothed over. It is as if the

two, inextricably intertwined by contrary principles, need to prop each other up for fear of the basic concept of the fence falling over for good. The fence as an entity may not be beautiful, but this does not disqualify it as a built form worthy of preservation. Its harsh reality may be the chief reason for preserving it.

PART 3: WINDMILL

THE DUST BOWL of the 1930s had been in the making since the 1870s, when industrialization began remaking the Great Plains in its own image: fencing, breaking up the old landscape; drilling, planting, cultivating, harvesting the new. By the turn of the twentieth century, the horses of buffalo hunting Indians and of cattle herding cowboys had been replaced by the power machinery of grain producing farmers. Barbed wire

fencing made the 160-acre homestead possible, but it required the development of mass produced, mass marketed windmills to make it habitable. The prairie wind was, is a fundamental fact of life and of death here.

Chicago, Illinois, 1893: "At the World's Columbia Exposition people see Edison's phonograph and other new mechanical and electrical wonders, but sunlight glinting from the sails of dozens of windmills pumping great streams of water make wind machines one of the fair's brightest

Exhibit of windmills at the 1893 World's Columbian Exposition.

sights... One wheel opens to get more wind or shuts against too much; another goes swiftly in the slightest breeze and, according to its manufacturer, works even in a tornado!" What excited the imagination of the writer of this account as well as fairgoers was not so much the spectacle of sunlight glinting from the spinning fans of these machines as the sight of the streams of water they were continuously and automatically pumping from the wells drilled beneath them.

Meade County, Kansas, late 1890s: This is a semi-arid region; the yearly average rainfall is less than 20 inches. Further, this limited amount of rain is not distributed evenly throughout the area, nor does the same amount fall each year. Seen in isolation,

however, the problem appeared a small blot on the expanse of treeless, rock-free, fertile land that stretched out before the plows of eager homesteaders.

"This," said a newcomer to the Plains, "would be fine country if it just had enough water."

"Yes," muttered the gaunt figure perched on a wagon headed back east, "so would hell."

The oldtimer had come here in the late 1880s and had joined up with three others planning to homestead. Each had filed on the regulation quarter-section of 160 acres, but they had decided to pool their limited personal resources to settle and then work the land. In the center, where the quarters met, they erected a sod house on one quarter, stables on two others, and located the all-important well on the fourth. "This was a good piece of work with water 140 feet below the surface," the oldtimer muttered, "and putting up that windmill was another." Perhaps thinking of repeatedly climbing the windmill tower to adjust or repair the mill after having dug out the sod with which they built the house, the oldtimer smiled grimly and observed, "Out here folks climb for water and dig for wood." Above the spot chosen for the well the four homesteaders had set up a rig that consisted of two timbers leaning against one another, a pulley about 15 feet above the ground, cables, and a heavy drill bit. Time after time they raised the bit, released it, worked a hole a little deeper into the earth, poured in some water, lowered a bailer, and hauled

35

the earth and water mixture to the surface. After reaching the ground water table, they drove in an iron casing to prevent the well from caving in. "We didn't lose the hole or drill bit or even the bailer," mused the oldtimer, who recalled a letter from those hopeful days in the box of relics lodged under the wagon seat:

I am glad to hear of your success in getting so much water. I am afraid it is too good to last, but hope it will.

Yes, it had been a good piece of work, and it was followed by another, even more demanding challenge: erection of a windmill tower.

The tower was built horizontally as an elongated pyramid about 16 feet square at the base, 20 feet tall. It was built with milled timber that had become available with the advent of the railroad; its corner posts, about 4 inches square, were connected laterally and diagonally with boards 2 inches thick. Near the apex of the pyramid a platform, roughly 6 feet square, was constructed as a place to grease or repair the mill, and a ladder was attached.

Now the tower had to be raised into position over the well -- again, "a good piece of work" given the limited tools and materials at hand. Four holes for the corner posts were dug, "deadmen" timbers to which wooden anchor pieces had been attached were buried, and then two of the tower legs were loosely bolted to anchors. After a snubbing post was erected and a cable attached to the top

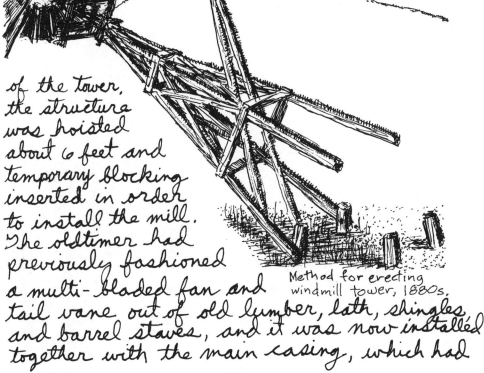

of the tower, the structure was hoisted about 6 feet and temporary blocking inserted in order to install the mill. The oldtimer had previously fashioned a multi-bladed fan and tail vane out of old lumber, lath, shingles and barrel staves, and it was now installed together with the main casing, which had

Method for erecting windmill tower, 1880s.

been salvaged from a derelict windmill. Again utilizing the snubbing point, hoisting cable, and the pulling power of draft animals, the completed assembly could now be lifted to its vertical position. The oldtimer had made certain that it was properly aligned over the well by lowering a window sash weight from the apex of the tower; the necessary adjustments were made, and then the four legs were bolted firmly to the anchor posts. It was a grand moment when the four builders cupped their hands under the cool water as it began gushing from the pipe below the tower; the oldtimer could still recall the taste of that first sweet drink.

Meade County, Kansas, late 1920s: "Does the wind blow like this all the time?" asked the visitor. "No," answered the farmer, "it'll maybe blow like this for a week or so and then it'll take a change and blow like hell."

As long as the native buffalo grass protected the Plains, the wind blew but the land did not, except in limited areas in

which the soil was unusually light or poorly anchored with a thin covering of grass.
With the advent of mechanized farming this ecological balance was thrown to the winds.

Each acre of sod traversed by roaring tractors, broken by steel plows, planted with mass produced grain drills, harvested with mass marketed headers and binders equaled that much less deeply rooted grass that could help the rich top soil resist the persistent gales. "And then there was the sound of a bent blade of our all-metal windmill as it encountered the tower with each revolution," a local historian recalled, "a machine-gun rattle in the gale that sent dust and dead weeds racing across the flat only to tangle together at the first line of barbed wire." The First World War had boosted wheat prices, and the government had proclaimed, "Wheat Will Win the War!" Meade County farmers had responded by breaking more sod to plant more wheat, and when prices tumbled in the 1920s, they had broken even more to expand production in compensation for the reduced profit margin.

Meade County, Kansas, late 1930s: Daylight is coming, but the farmer is still seated at the table, writing in the thick notebook that has been the only witness of his lonely struggle over the past eight years:

I dare not venture out into the swirling dust which has done away with all visibility. Vividly before my eyes I can picture my wheat crop hanging in the balance. Some of it has doubtless been ruined in the night, but I am confident that most of it survives. If only the wind would slacken now, I would yet have a crop, but if the gale continues until noon, I can see no hope for my wheat.

Night has fallen; the farmer is again seated at the table writing:

It continued to blow until noon and long after; and the thermometer of my hopes has reached a new low, for now I see all my crop gone, and I feel utterly discouraged and sick at heart. No longer is there need for me to care how long or how hard the wind might blow, since whereas, only yesterday my prospects seemed brighter than they ever had been since I started to farm the Dust Bowl, there is now nothing left for me but to give up, accept utter defeat, and move away from here.

Southern plains, late 1970s: Hundreds of feet beneath the dry surface lies a fresh-water aquifer that extends from western Nebraska to southern Texas. A windmill can not generate enough energy to raise this water. It requires a powerful centrifugal pump and a new type of center-pivoting irrigation system, which has transformed the landscape from a giant checkerboard to crossing rows of irrigated checkers. At the rate

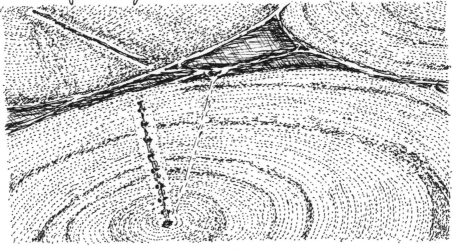

the aquifer is being depleted it is predicted that this resource will run dry within the first decades of the approaching century.

"I don't think that will happen," a farmer insists. "And if it does we'll get more water from someplace else... There's no way the Dust Bowl could happen again. We've got the machinery to stop it."

A water pumping windmill patterned after a wind-powered electric generator.

The Land Institute, Salina, Kansas, early 1980s: The two interns had determined that the windmill needed a few repairs and decided to take on the job themselves. It did not take them long to discover that there was little printed information useful to them as novices, but that a couple who sold and serviced a similar type of windmill in a city nearby would be pleased to help them.

After examining old manuals and the parts of a disassembled windmill

42

at the couple's workshop, the novices had a
better idea of the problem confronting them
and how to go about solving it: the heavy
superstructure would have to be disconnected from the tower and lowered to
the ground for close inspection and the
small, but important repairs that were
required—— a dangerous procedure
that needed a boom truck. The couple
offered to visit the farm and the use of
their truck.

　"When they came, it was a great
event," an intern recalled. "Everyone
at The Land Institute came by to have a
look and listen to their explanations."
By the end of the day, the mill was
repaired and ready to be hooked up to
the well, which had been cleaned for
the occasion.

　The interns had learned that this
could be done at some cost with compressed
air or at no cost with an old-fashioned
bailer. The bailer they had opted to use
was a pipe, four feet long and three
inches in diameter, with a one-way

valve at the bottom. Time after time they had lowered it to the bottom of the well where upon impact it had filled with silt and sand; time after time they had hauled the bailer up and emptied it out.

Gazing at the spinning fan of the windmill, which was working better for having been raised in the process of being repaired, the intern explained, "The Land Institute is a non-profit organization devoted to a search for sustainable alternatives to the form of farming that produced the Dust Bowl, which is its most dramatic and dramatized, but far from its most destructive consequence."

"Grass Variations" for 5 dancers in 13 sections as performed at an event co-sponsored by The Land Institute (1982).

SOURCES

Part 1

Adorno, Theodor. Aesthetic Theory. London:
　　Routledge and Kegan Paul, 1986.
Banham, Reyner. A Concrete Atlantis. Cambridge:
　　The MIT Press, 1986.
Le Corbusier. Towards a New Architecture.
　　London: The Architectural Press, 1946.
Freivalds, John. Grain Trade. New York:
　　Stein and Day, 1976.
Morgan, Dan. Merchants of Grain. New York:
　　Viking Press, 1979.
Rudofsky, Bernard. Architecture Without
　　Architects. New York: Museum of
　　Modern Art, 1965.

Part 2

Day, Samuel, Jr. Nuclear Heartland. Madison,
　　Wisconsin: The Progressive Foundation,
　　1988.
McGrath, Thomas. Passages Toward the Dark.
　　Townsend, Washington: Copper Canyon
　　Press, 1982.
Muilenburg, G. and Swineford, A. Land
　　of the Post Rock. Lawrence, Kansas,
　　University Press of Kansas, 1975.
Piper, E. F. Barbed Wire and Other Poems.
　　The Midland Press, 1917 (not located).
Webb, W.P. The Great Plains. Lincoln, Nebraska:
　　University of Nebraska Press, 1959.

Part 3

Baker, T.L. A Field Guide to American
　　Windmills. Norman, Oklahoma: The
　　University of Oklahoma Press, 1985.

Evans, Jerry. "Prairie Images," The Land
    Report (Salina, Kansas), Summer, 1982.
Hirschberg, Lynn. "Restoring the Water
    Pumping Windmill," The Land Report,
    Summer, 1982.
Svoboda, Lawrence. Farming the Dust Bowl.
    Lawrence, Kansas: University Press
    of Kansas, 1986.
Worster, Donald. Dust Bowl: The Southern
    Plains in the 1930s. New York: Oxford
    University Press, 1979.

HOUSE, SCHOOLHOUSE, HOUSE (continued)

"You're given just so much to work with in life, and you have to do the best you can with what you've got," a nineteenth century quilter wrote. "The material is passed on to you or is all you can afford... That's just what's given you. Your fate. But the way you put the pieces together is your business."

PART I

SOD HOUSE. From a letter written by a Kansas homesteader in the mid-1870s:
He thought he could make room for me in the tiny dugout until I had a place to sleep on my claim. My traps were deposited in a corner, and after resting a bit, I struck out to look for "corners" of my claim about 3/4 mile away, which I did not succeed in finding -- so here I am fixed for a few days...

Besides the crowding -- the three people already there had to share the only bed -- there were other difficulties: bed bugs and fleas, flies and mosquitoes swarmed in the earthen structure with no screens; food was poor, the surface water that was drunk was unsanitary; clothing was inadequate, and there was little opportunity to wash anything.

This is a sod house [the letter continues], for sod is the most available material, in fact, the only material the homesteader has, unless he happens to be one who secured a creek with timber suitable for logs. Perhaps you will be interested

49

in the way it is built...

The following description of the building practice is assembled from a number of letters.

Foundation: I staked the two corners of my claim [and] found a spot to make a dugout at the head of the prettiest draw on my claim, laid off the ground 10 x 14 feet, and began to dig... Talk about hard work will you? Just try digging in the ground out here two feet from the surface -- oh, I should have written 6 inches from the surface. The ground is packed just as hard as could be, and it is no fun to pick and shovel it. It is damp as far as I have gone down (about 27 inches) and sticky as putty...

Wall construction: The builder usually lays up a single layer of sods, though sometimes he crosses two layers, which makes the wall about two feet thick... When the ground is thoroughly soaked by rain or snow is the best time for breaking sod for building... Slices of sod 2½ inches wide, are cut with a sharp spade into 18-inch lengths then laid up... Care must be taken to stagger joints and bind the corners of the wall; it is likely to settle a good deal, because the sod is

50

usually very wet when laid. The door and window frames are set in place and the wall built around them.

Roof construction: When the four walls are in place, the crotches (tree forks) are set at the ends and in the middle of the room, and the ridgepole -- a tree trunk, sometimes spliced, running the length of the building is raised into place...

Wooden poles and air space left for settling of sod above board window frame.

One morning after I dug out the steps, I struck for [a friend's place] to get my ridgepole. He had timber for sale, and after looking at some trees struck a bargain for one 14 to 16 inches through at the butt and about 20 feet clear of branches for #1. They cut it down, lopped the top off 18 feet from the butt, and hauled it to my claim for an additional 50¢...

Ridge pole supported by crotch at gable end (usually within house).

Loading that log was no easy work, and we almost broke the wagon trying; so [we decided] just to tie the log to the hind

51

wheels and drag it on the ground. [The next day I returned] to cut up the top of that tree into pieces handy to haul...

After the ridgepole is raised, poles are laid from the ridge to the walls and covered with any available material -- straight sorghum stalks, willow switches and straw, anything that will prevent the sod on the roof from falling between the rafters. In the middle, from the top of the ridgepole to the floor is little more than 7 feet, under the eaves the height is about 6 feet. The gables are finished -- and the roof covered with sod.

← sod

← wild grass

← brush

← pole

← beam

SOD ROOF

Finishing: At first sod houses are unplastered, and this is thought perfectly alright, but crevices between the sods admit cold in winter -- so [at a later date] the houses are plastered with [a mixture of] sand and a very sticky native clay. [In a few cases] the plaster is white washed, and this helps the looks very much. [Well built]

sod houses are mighty comfortable places...
and don't take much fire to keep them warm.
I will have to be contented with a very
modest affair for a while, but perhaps
can improve it later...

Furniture: The interior is as
follows -- a door and window (east wall); a
pile of potatoes (corner); a stove (against
the north wall) and tin boiler, etc. (in the
adjacent corner); trunks and sack of flour
(against the west wall); the bed (southwest
corner); a box, on top of which is a
store box converted into a cupboard
(corner next to door). The letter that
contains this information provides a
diagrammatic floor plan indicating
"valises" in an area where the reader
might expect to see the otherwise
unmentioned table and chairs.

The absence of fuel storage from the
description suggests an even more serious
problem. Wood in the region was scarce
and coal expensive. "Dead sunflowers made
a good fire and burned longer than corn-
stalks. Cow chips were another kind of
fuel," a local historian reported. "About

53

all one person could do was keep fire..." a popular joke of the time tells of a man who upon being asked about his family replies, "the children are alright but I hardly know about my wife since ours is a passing acquaintance. We see each other only as she is going out with a pan of ashes and I am coming in with a bucket of cow chips."

Cooking and dining under such conditions posed other challenges. A homesteader recalled, "Occasionally Mother had to cook while one of us held an umbrella over the food to keep mud and rain-water from dripping into the pot." Another typical problem produced this joke; "With company sitting about awaiting the meal, Mother was chagrined and embarrassed to suddenly realize there were more people than knives. She remarked to my sister --so that the company might hear, 'My goodness, Sal, where are all our knives gone to?' Sal, unaware of Mother's newfound concern as a hostess replied, 'Why Ma, they're all here: Big Butch, Little Butch, Case and Stub.'"

PART 2

SCHOOLHOUSE.

Northeastern Kansas, late–20th century: A limestone structure built in 1871 with remnants of its wood roof is located on the northern boundary of a state park

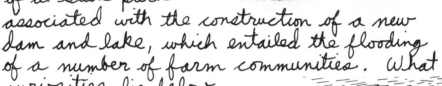

associated with the construction of a new dam and lake, which entailed the flooding of a number of farm communities. What curiosities lie below the surface of a lake whose deepest water is reserved for artifacts that were once commonplace? Severed from earlier associations, the artifacts lie there like relics in a vast tomb. In memory, we advance from a small, inconsequential

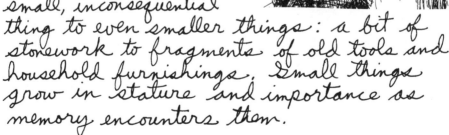

thing to even smaller things: a bit of stonework to fragments of old tools and household furnishings. Small things grow in stature and importance as memory encounters them.

I recall a short story by Willa Cather, "The Best Years," whose protagonist is a "County Superintendent of Public Instruction " in Nebraska about the time the Barber School opened its door as a one-room schoolhouse.

A grim title, that, to put upon a charming young woman [Cather writes]. Fortunately it was seldom used... She is not even called 'Super-indendent.' A county schoolteacher said to her pupils; ' I think Miss Knightly will come to see us this week. She was at Walnut Creek yesterday.'

Presently she arrives at a schoolhouse... When Miss Knightly stopped before the door, a boy ran out to hand her from the buggy and to take care of [the mare]. The little teacher stood on the doorstep... Miss Knightly took her arm, and they went into the schoolroom.

After Miss Knightly listens to a lesson and the teacher sends the children outdoors, the two sit down on a bench in the corner of the room to talk. "I'm very well satisfied," Miss Knightly says. She suggests they share a lunch she brought and then "hear the advanced arithmetic class."

While the pupils were doing their sums at the blackboard [the story continues], Miss Knightly herself was doing a little

56

figuring. This was Thursday. Tomorrow she would visit two schools, and she had planned to spend Friday night with a pleasant family on Farmer's Creek. But she could change her schedule...

During the recess following the lesson, the Superintendent discloses her plan:

I've been wondering, Lesley, whether you wouldn't like to go back to town with me after school tomorrow... and you could have all of Saturday and Sunday at home. Then we would make an early start on Monday morning, and I would drop you here at the schoolhouse...

Lesley happily agrees, and the reader meets her family. The story explores the family relationships in some detail, then shifts focus: Miss Knightly is in Lincoln at a later date, attending a convention when a "long-to-be-remembered blizzard swept down over the state." She is snowbound until train service is resumed a week later. On the train she "is pleased to see Mr. Redman in conductor's uniform come into the car," and they are soon talking about the storm:

This has taught us we just can't handle an emergency [he explains]. Hard on stock, hard on people. A little neighbor of ours -- why, you must know her, she was one of your teachers... She got pneumonia in the country and died out there.

57

It is Lesley. Upon learning this, "Miss Knightly went so white" that the conductor became concerned. "That's all right, Mr. Redman," Miss Knightly reassures him. "Did she get lost in the storm? I don't understand."

"No, Ma'am, little Lesley acted very sensible, didn't lose her head." The conductor describes how the storm suddenly closed in on "the little schoolroom" and how the students "jumped up to run out, but Lesley stood with her back against the door and wouldn't let 'em go out." Afternoon turned to evening. At a nearby farm, a farmer, after much effort to minimize damage and loss, enters his house...

As soon as he got in [Mr. Redman explains], the missus made him go over to the school-house an' take a rope along an' herd 'em all over to her house, teacher an' all...

They stay the night. The next day "fathers came on horseback for the children." Lesley, however, seemed "pretty sick," and died three days later.

Cather's story concludes with Miss Knightly, who has moved to New England like Cather herself, returning to Nebraska to revisit scenes and people that she has been thinking about for years.

As usual at the time that the Barber School was built, it was given the name of the family who had donated a portion of their farmland for the construction of a schoolhouse -- in this case, in memory of the first local victim of anti-slavery struggles that culminated in "Bleeding Kansas" and the Civil War. An unpaved county road pushes its way past the

north side of the schoolhouse -- rising, falling, calling forth details of the landscape that would have been critical to a Civil War commander deploying soldiers -- here a rock outcropping and distant view, there a hollow of entangled foliage. An active quarry intrudes upon the northeast corner of the site and a power line upon the east end of the building. South and west of the structure a field of native grasses and wildflowers gropes its way upwards towards a blinding sun.

Little remains of the original schoolhouse. Half of the western wall is missing together with an adjacent

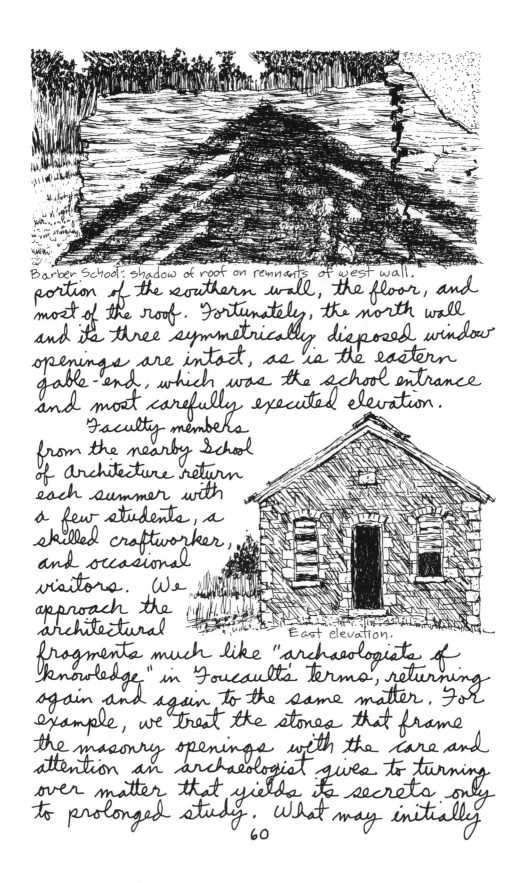

Barber School: shadow of roof on remnants of west wall.

portion of the southern wall, the floor, and most of the roof. Fortunately, the north wall and its three symmetrically disposed window openings are intact, as is the eastern gable-end, which was the school entrance and most carefully executed elevation.

Faculty members from the nearby School of Architecture return each summer with a few students, a skilled craftworker, and occasional visitors. We approach the architectural

East elevation.

fragments much like "archaeologists of knowledge" in Foucault's terms, returning again and again to the same matter. For example, we treat the stones that frame the masonry openings with the care and attention an archaeologist gives to turning over matter that yields its secrets only to prolonged study. What may initially

60

appear as crude stone-work around a doorway or window reveals subtle refinements over time.

What makes the very first glimpse of the eroded structure incomparable is an aura of desolation mixed with unexpected feelings of connection between the piled stones and waving grasses, roof timbers and an enormous sky. We note things as they appear at first glance in sketch pads, but with caution -- each pen stroke made like the probe of an archaeological spade. The initial sketch can be blurred, even blotted out with a few scribbled second thoughts, for it is hard to keep sight of what is initially seen as a unity. For example, the subtle relationships between the north wall and its openings can be overly simplified by an outline drawing, which can establish false boundaries between wall and masonry opening, what is inside and what is outside the structure.

As with any "dig," investigative and recording procedures have been established. Each stone and roofing timber

is patiently noted as well as each connection,
especially those which have been broken,
such as the connection indicated by Cather
that once existed between the schoolhouse and
the teacher, students, and families who
all lived within a four mile radius. The
objective of this procedure is to note in
what ways the schoolhouse is like others
of its kind and in what ways it is
irreducible to any other structure --
that is, the objective is to define the
Barber School in its specificity. The
focus of this effort is not the sequence
of school building and education policies
in Kansas during the years the structure
functioned as a one-teacher school:
from the period following the Civil War
to the end of the Second World War.
Rather, the focus is on how these
policies were made manifest in the
construction, periodic repair, abandonment,
and final neglect of the structure itself.
For example, in the early decades of the
20th century the ideas of John Dewey and

like-minded educators began to filter into structures such as the Barber School. Revising the curriculum entailed rethinking the layout and design of the school's exterior as well as interior facilities, and indications of such alterations are, by their very nature, an aspect of our investigation.

A record of this type of investigation does not resemble a report and even less a chronological list. Rather, it is more like a stack of notations sketched on mismatched bits of tracing paper. The investigator must probe fragments of building activity, arrange and rearrange scraps of information. The tool is a variable. Only when the precision of a proposed intervention directly influences the shape of the project can the computer be allowed to alienate hand from pen, for it replaces the pliancy of the moving arm with the rigidity of mechanical commands.

West wall at ridge.

South wall opening.

Those of us working on the Barber School have come up with a few rules-of-thumb:

(1) Be adventurous, and having investigated one area, explore paths that might lead to an unmapped patch of ground.

(2) Seek out vantage points which are unfamiliar and uncomfortable. While the latter acts as a grindstone that sharpens the investigative pick, the former focuses attention on what might be considered unimportant and casually cast aside.

(3) Record each stage of the investigation. Utilize a mixture of media and avoid anything resembling a standard format. An abundance of things noted is indispensable. Let a growing urge to assemble the pieces act as a goad for completion.

(4) Keep the recording pen aloof from the temptation to quickly outline an architectural feature that seems uninspired or poorly executed. Examine such a detail with special attention, and redraw what is already drawn using another scale or graphic medium. Insight may awaken in the process.

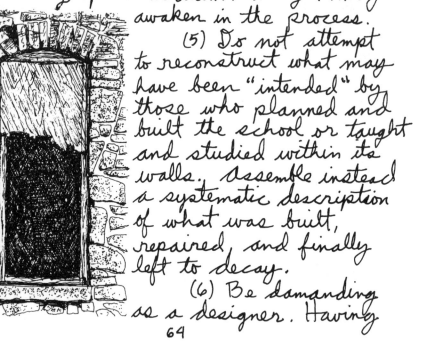

(5) Do not attempt to reconstruct what may have been "intended" by those who planned and built the school or taught and studied within its walls. Assemble instead a systematic description of what was built, repaired, and finally left to decay.

(6) Be demanding as a designer. Having

completed a series of tracings, shift the vantage point from past to future and do another series. This shift opens up the investigation and brings the question of preservation into focus: to restore or rehabilitate the Barber School?

FLOOR PLAN, reuse study

We make a distinction between a proposal to reconstruct architectural features that are no longer there, such as a missing wall section, for example, and one that builds upon what is still visible, such as the roof profile. Any preservation effort intersects with both architectural continuity and change, traditional and innovative building procedures. We try to describe these relationships and interdependencies in design proposals. Different types and degrees of disconnection from the existing fragments begin to emerge.

We have found that this form of investigation and the proposals it generates resemble what Foucault called a "tree of derivation of a discourse." At the bottom: a deformed and structurally defective foundation of particular dimensions, examined and recorded stone-by-stone. At the top: an emergence of conceptual transformations and technical improvements,

65

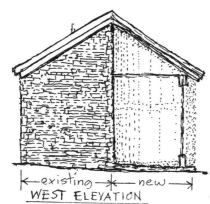

├←existing→│← new →│
WEST ELEVATION

an architectural burgeoning that excludes any semblance of purity.

Preservationists tend to credit the buildings they wish to restore with stylistic cohesion. If they notice an irregularity, they look for a principle of organization and invest the procedure with a name. For example, the remaining fragments of the roof of the Barber School indicate that it had been built and/or repaired with scraps of framing lumber patched together in a triangular shape that a preservation official referred to as a "king-post truss." He then faulted any proposal that did not adhere to this "principle." Further, he wanted us to believe that this ruling was a procedural obligation, a legal constraint of "Historic Preservation."

We have argued that there is no textbook system to be identified. The odd assortment of lumber and ways of connecting the pieces together should be recognized for what they were: a making-do with what was available. Nothing could be more counter-productive than to start reading into

SECTION at entry

Top of wall.

these fragments the name of some structural "system," architectural "style," or "period" of architectural history.

The official disagreed: Not too much weight should be given to deviations from the norm nor should small differences be exaggerated. Rather, a principle of cohesion should be found at a deeper level of analysis, and the Barber School restored to its original conceptual unity. In order to reconstruct this unity, its existence first has to be assumed, then found and properly identified. This procedure also had a name: "research."

Nevertheless, we have had to make-do with what is available: a random assortment of donated building materials, a few tools, limited skills, and unlimited enthusiasm. The situation is further complicated by the academic nature of the project: an eight-week summer course scheduled to meet three mornings a week, which requires studio work and field trips as well as a building practicum. Many of us have appeared the other two weekday mornings as well, but we have been able to accomplish only so much. First, the masonry had to be stabilized, which

meant buttressing the weakest sections of the foundation and repointing the stonework. Then we had to find a way to support a new roof without altering the existing sections of the wall; to make them structurally dependable would be a costly and technically complex undertaking.

While the walls were being stabilized, a suggestion of adding interior columns to support the roof was hotly debated and then accepted as a working hypothesis. Various design proposals raised a basic question about the nature of the intervention: should it entail a similar or contrasting building technology? masonry and wood or crisply detailed steel? Unfortunately, the debate lasted only as long as the donation of steel columns seemed a possibility. While making a mock-up of a column shaft and pedestal with materials lying about the site, the next and ultimately

Digging trench for buttressing foundation at northwest corner.

Rebuilding the northwest corner.

Diagram of concept and perspective of mock-up.

most important hypothesis was formulated:
to build with available resources, anonymously
and communally. "Surely, this was the way
the schoolhouse was built and might get
itself rebuilt," the craftworker observed.

Upon learning of this development,
the preservation official became uneasy and
referred to "federal guidelines," which
contained no such hypothesis, but rather,
clearly stated "standards." We soon agreed,
however, that arguing about different
interpretations of those standards would
not achieve anything but mutual ill-will;
furthermore, there was a basic difference
underlying the ongoing friction between the
official and us: the difference between
our architectural formulations, which he
found fuzzy-minded, and the official's
pronouncements, which we felt were
simple-minded. This was not necessarily
a difference between Historic Preservation
and Architecture as professions, for it

69

manifests itself within the professions themselves: between one body of preservation theory and another, between one architectural practice and another. For example, compare our architectural "rules-of-thumb" with the following comment and drawing, which come from from a study of rural and urban house types by a respected architect --

The intent of this investigation is dual: first, it reviews a diversity of American house types; second, it pursues an understanding of simple, idiosyncratic house forms for underlying typological and conceptual principles...

one room   stack   two door   saddlebag   "I" type

and this from the concluding notes of the same study:

Geometric simplicity is a persistent and unwavering characteristic which can be seen in even the most basic house form. With two doors, two windows and a fireplace, the one room house is a picture of geometric clarity, its cube form crisply cut into the steep triangular gable of the roof. Windows and doors are subordinated to the mass, being cut directly into it without elaboration around the openings...

This is the way this architect (Steven Holl) has chosen to present vernacular house types, which is to reduce them to a series of diagrammatic outline drawings. Curiously, with a few minor corrections this same description could be mistakenly applied to the one-room Barber School. Even more curious, compare this reductive analytic procedure to the "relentlessly examining" procedure adopted by the same architect in his own practice, as described below by an architectural critic:

one teacher

Steven Holl says that his firm worked on [the design of a house built in Texas in the early 1990s] for seven months before the clients saw any drawings or models, and later refined the design for an additional eight months. The time and care invested show in the intricately crafted decorations that link motifs and proportions at every scale... interlocking paradigms of movement and repose... a system built on almost total self-referentiality... near-obsessive use of golden-section relationships... a second set of references, based on the free curves of the roof... This list is far from exhaustive. All the surfaces and even what lies beneath them have been drafted into the service of Holl's relentlessly examining... [his own

DALLAS: Texas Stretto House. View of "cascading roofs" from living room.

71

design], but not "the diversity of American house types." Where the preservation official unnecessarily complicates the analysis of vernacular architecture, Holl over-simplifies it. In short, the difference between simple-minded and fuzzy-minded architectural formulations exists not only between and in professional disciplines, but also within the body of work produced by this exemplary architect.

Barber School, summer 1994.

PART 3

BALLOON FRAME

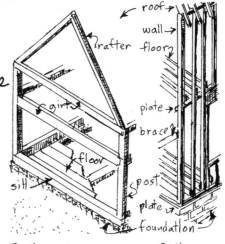

Timber frame (18th century).

Balloon frame.

construction was dependent on two developments: the mass production of round, sharply pointed wire, later steel nails and standardized lumber milled with steam-driven saws. Both the prairie houses designed by Frank Lloyd Wright and farmhouses built in the Great Plains from the end of the 19th century through the first decade of the 20th century share family resemblances and lend themselves to being grouped into a few diagrammatic types, much like the procedure Steven Holl applies to his study of vernacular houses (with similar limitations).

 A recent study of farmhouses begins with a rectangle, called either "type 1 or 2" (depending on the number of stories.) This shape is echoed in a study by a scholar of Wright's house plans who calls it "in-line" or "wall" (depending on site conditions):

FARMHOUSE: Type 2

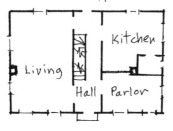

WRIGHT: Wall type (1891).

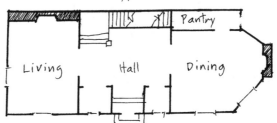

an addition of a wing to a rectangular farmhouse generates "ell" and "T-shaped" floor plans, while the prairie house has its own type of "T-plan:"

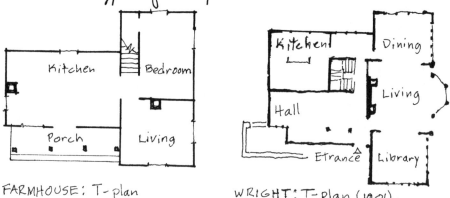

FARMHOUSE: T-plan   WRIGHT: T-plan (1901)

The addition of a wing to either side of the base rectangle forms a "cross," which appears as "cruciform" to the student of Wrights' work:

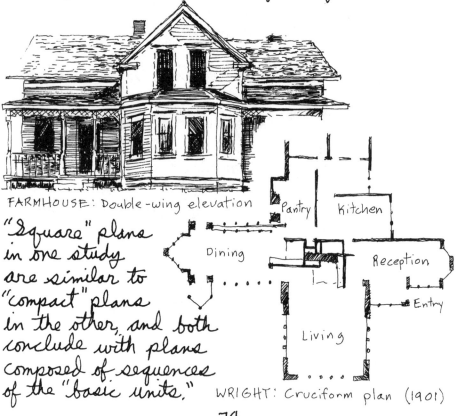

FARMHOUSE: Double-wing elevation

"Square" plans in one study are similar to "compact" plans in the other, and both conclude with plans composed of sequences of the "basic units."

WRIGHT: Cruciform plan (1901)

74

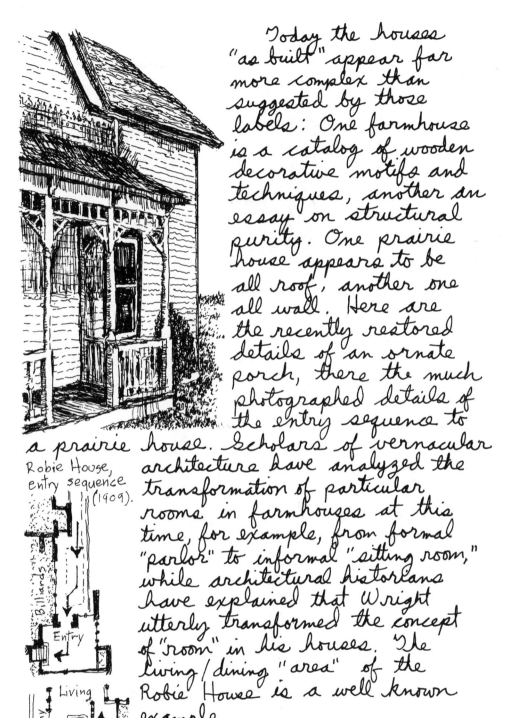

Robie House,
entry sequence
(1909).

Billiards

Entry

Living

Balcony

Dining

Today the houses "as built" appear far more complex than suggested by those labels: One farmhouse is a catalog of wooden decorative motifs and techniques, another an essay on structural purity. One prairie house appears to be all roof, another one all wall. Here are the recently restored details of an ornate porch, there the much photographed details of the entry sequence to a prairie house. Scholars of vernacular architecture have analyzed the transformation of particular rooms in farmhouses at this time, for example, from formal "parlor" to informal "sitting room," while architectural historians have explained that Wright utterly transformed the concept of "room" in his houses. The living/dining "area" of the Robie House is a well known example.

The challenge is to neither exaggerate nor diminish the importance of these features,

75

but to observe and evaluate them as built; to cut through the formulation of oppositions: between unique and commonplace architecture, one and many of a kind, spectacular and banal, true architectural imagination and

Robie House, view from living to dining.

false. For example, most commentators agree that the concept of "room" in Wright's prairie-house designs represents a creative breakthrough. Some insist that the development was the product of Wright's untrammeled imagination. Other commentators trace it to his exposure to traditional Japanese architecture, especially Ho-o-den, which he must have seen at the World's Columbian Exposition in Chicago; or to his awareness of one-room houses built by homesteaders, while others relate it to social theories and experiments he heard at Chicago's Hull-House. Any one or combination of these explanations may be true -- or

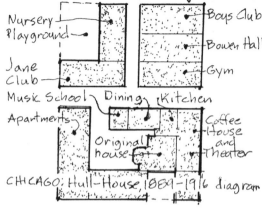

Nursery
Playground
Jane Club
Music School
Apartments
Boys Club
Bowen Hall
Gym
Dining   Kitchen
Original house
Coffee House and Theater

CHICAGO: Hull-House, 1889-1916 diagram

none of them. Whether Wright was inventing or imitating the concept of "room" as an integration of various activities within a subtly divided spatial volume is far less significant than the fact that such a concept entered or reentered the field of building practice in the region at this time. Within the next fifty years both plain and fancy houses were being built less as an addition of functionally defined, separate rooms and more as an ensemble of smaller spatial units furnished for specific activities such as plugging new electronic equipment into a multi-purpose "family room."

> Willa Cather lived in Red Cloud [Nebraska] from 1884 (age 11) to 1890 (age 17) when she went to Lincoln State University. She herself said that the first years of life make the deepest impression, and she relived those Red Cloud years in each of her Nebraska books.
> from The World of Willa Cather
> by Mildred R. Bennett

During the final years of her life, Mildred Bennett gave me the opportunity to coordinate a series of projects in and around Red Cloud related to preservation efforts spearheaded by the Willa Cather Memorial and Educational Foundation, of which she was president and guiding spirit. One of these projects was a farmhouse described in several works by Cather, but most important to the

Foundation as the home of the title character
in the novel My Antonia. In 1987 Joan Stone
choreographed a dance, Sweet Home, and
wrote narration for a recorded score,
which dramatized an incident in the novel.
Its performance at the Third National Willa
Cather Seminar by a dance group Joan
directed, brought us together with Mildred
Bennett at the seminar, later in Red Cloud,
and eventually in the Foundation's preservation
work. My attitude towards architectural
preservation in Red Cloud was anticipated
in the opening words of the narration that
accompanied the dance:
"Life can't stand still even
in the quietest of country
towns." I perceived my
relationship to the people
and buildings of Red Cloud
to be something like that of
the Mrs. Vanni of the
narrative: "Mrs. Vanni
worked in Kansas City in
the winter, and in the
summer traveled to small

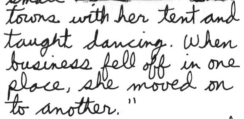

towns with her tent and
taught dancing. When
business fell off in one
place, she moved on
to another."

"You're given just
so much to work with
in life, and you have
to do the best you can

with what you've got," a 19th century quilter wrote. "The material is passed on to you or is all you can afford... That's just what's given you. Your fate. But the way you put the pieces together is your business." This was the spirit in which Sweet Home was choreographed; the words apply equally well to architectural preservation, especially our work in Red Cloud. The Foundation had obtained the home of Annie and John Pavelka (Antonia's home at the end of the novel) and deeded it to the Nebraska State Historical Society. Both organizations wished to have it recorded, placed on the National Register of Historic Places, and a suitable use found for it. Most pressing was the need for a set of measured drawings that my students were pleased to contribute.

Pavelka farmhouse entrance

The house began as a two-room, one-story rectangular structure with a gable roof. It was moved to its existing location in 1911 at which time it was transformed into an ell-shape, popular at the time, by attaching a story-and-a half addition with a clipped gable roof and dormers.

original structure | additions

Pavelka farmhouse, entrance elevation.

This structure was subsequently "modernized," a process that utterly changed the character of the structure known to Willa Cather. It was easy enough to record, but the notion of removing the "modern" additions and turning a "restored" farmhouse into a museum, which was a possibility being given serious consideration, raised difficult questions for the students: Could, should time be reversed? What would be the best way of "deconstructing" the structure and making such a procedure visible? What about the farm itself and landscaping? Again, could time be reversed? Furnishings: this issue raised innumerable questions, especially about reproducing "period" rooms. All these questions seemed to gravitate about a central issue: tourism.

It seemed unlikely that tourists conditioned to expect theme-park entertainment could be tempted to examine

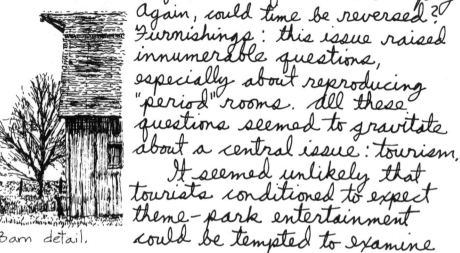

Barn detail.

the various stages of construction and modification of this remote and ungainly farmhouse. There are a limited number of people who consider a literary pilgrimage to be an appropriate vacation activity, but their interests would not necessarily coincide with the proposed restoration project. "A Cather pilgrimage -- to her home town, for instance -- can be interesting," a scholar has explained, "but like most literary pilgrimages, has ultimately not much to do with a reading of her novels. It is an inner, not an outer journey that's required... Being led by kindly guides around the 'Cather Childhood Home' or the

RED CLOUD: Cather residence from 1884 to 1904.

'Cather Memorial Prairie' did not unlock, though it might illustrate 'Old Mrs Harris' or My Antonia..." It was easy to conclude that any adaptive reuse proposal was unrealistic, for the cost of even the most minimal intervention would exceed the structure's value as real estate or a tourist attraction. "Nonsense," Mildred Bennett exclaimed. "It is a wonderful place in which someone inspired by Cather,

81

perhaps a writer or painter, can live and work and gradually restore. We should give that person a chance -- and a few ideas..." These words accompanied by an inviting smile. My favorite proposal came from a student who simply added a few words to the measured floor plans: the initial two-room structure was designated as "work place," the addition as "home place," its ground floor identified as

GROUND FLOOR
original structure | additions

"directed outward" and upper story as "inward turning."

Mildred Bennett seemed to have an unlimited number of projects for us, a few of which we had the opportunity to complete: preparing a drawing with which a local builder might estimate the cost of reconstructing a steeple destroyed by lightning that had graced the Cather family church; measured drawings

RED CLOUD: Episcopal Church.

of a deteriorating commercial structure; archival work; various projects related to her dream of building a large meeting hall. Her health was failing, but not her spirit

82

and ability to inspire us. I was reminded of an episode in Sweet Home, an "angry galop":

The hired girls talked and thought of nothing but the dance pavilion [the script explained]. They hummed and practiced the steps all day... They hurried with their work, daydreamed, lingered too long talking and laughing. They were warned to quit going to those dances, or they could hunt other jobs... Stop going to the tent: they wouldn't think of it. People like them, they said, had to have their fling when they could. Maybe there wouldn't be a tent next year...

There wasn't -- either for Mildred Bennett or for our work in Red Cloud. The dance concluded with the dancers unweaving the streamers they had woven together in the middle of Sweet Home. The narration explained:

Jim noticed one afternoon that his grandmother had been crying. It was the dance pavilion.

83

She had heard things -- bad talk.

He argued that there was nothing wrong. He liked the hired girls, and he liked to dance. That was all there was to it.

He didn't care what people said about him, but if the talk hurt his grandmother, that settled it. He promised not to go to the tent again.

Such disapprobation dulled the enthusiasm for dancing, and the dance pavilion moved on before the end of the summer. It was considered a challenge to the social order. It was new and different...

Jim kept his promise. Back to sitting at home like an image or prowling about hunting for diversion. He made up his mind to get away as soon as possible... [the hired girls, too]... Mrs. Vanni packed up her dancing skirt, and the dance pavilion moved on.

Mildred Bennett's dream of transforming the Pavelka farmhouse into an artist's residence has faded into the past. The cultural stagnation that Cather anticipated, which drove the dance pavilion of her novel out of Red Cloud, is ascendent.

PART 4, HOUSE AS COMMODITY.

... Aladdin Homes, Sears-Roebuck, Southern Mill of Tulsa, Houston Ready-Cut, Montgomery Ward... By 1920, manufacturers had saturated the Great Plains with prefabricated houses, including a few with "Prairie-Style features" but without the slightest trace of the work of either Frank Lloyd Wright or the domestic reform movement that had been an influence on the Prairie Style.

The linch-pin of the contemporary house is the appearance of a sign in its neatly trimmed front yard that alternately announces: yard sale, garage sale, house for sale SOLD. What made this basic change in the concept of home is not simply words painted on a placard thrust into the ground, but the choice and placement of plant material, the design of a house that can accommodate automobiles and a recreation vehicle with boat in tow, many appliances, and much furniture. The basis of this building practice is transformation of people's needs, hopes,

85

and memories into objects that can be bought and sold -- on credit. Calculations by manufacturers of building equipment, materials, components, and power tools; real estate developers, agencies, and marketing firms; building contractors and sub-contractors; money lending institutions and people with monthly payments due on mortgages determine the location of the building, what both the landscape and house look like, how they are maintained, and the daily life they encompass. Fragmentation of the object of these calculations, the house, has entailed fragmentation of the subject--designer, builder, owner, user -- all of whom must conform to exactly defined, quantifiable functions. The only thing that gets property owners talking and acting as a group is something they fear might lower resale values in the area. A resident who has replaced lawn with native grasses receives a legal notice about a "Plant Ordinance." It is a building practice of short-term financial transactions.

Even a house built with an unlimited budget and little concern for its resale by people who are more or less aware of the stultifying influence that the housing market has on residential

Detail in the "Prairie School Tradition" (1976).

architecture may be coopted by the fashion industry as a showcase of luxury products.

Reduction of built form from the realm of architectural language to that of commercial jargon is effected by removing it from the context of history and, at the same time, reducing architecture

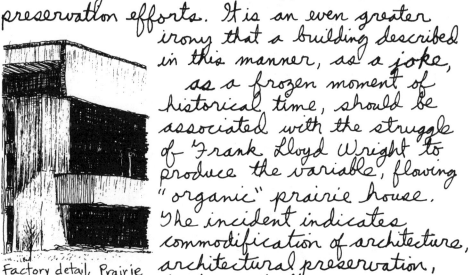

to a series of paraphrased, Michael Graves, a vanity. or worse, caricatured details... "The meeting will be held in one of those 'prairie-style' office buildings being built on the parkway," I was informed, "the one with the zig-zag roof and brickish facade with keystone-decal window frames..." Ironically the meeting concerned local architectural preservation efforts. It is an even greater irony that a building described in this manner, as a joke, as a frozen moment of historical time, should be associated with the struggle of Frank Lloyd Wright to produce the variable, flowing "organic" prairie house. The incident indicates commodification of architecture, architectural preservation, history itself...

Factory detail, Prairie School Tradition (1964).

87

and it is representative --

OPEN SUNDAY 1-3 PM   OPEN SUNDAY 1-3 PM

PRICE REDUCED TO $116,900 $92,900 FIRST TIME OPEN

QUALITY RANCHER!   For just $122,900   GREAT EAST SIDE LOCATION $189,900

Exploration, overland travel, homesteading, the cattle trade, railroad building, town founding... "And now four centuries from the discovery of America, at the end of a hundred years of life under the Constitution, the frontier has gone, and with its going has closed the first period of American history," proclaimed Frederick Jackson Turner. The year was 1893, and the World's Columbian Exposition in honor of "Columbus' discovery of the New World" proclaimed the opening of the new era. It was called "White City."

"There may be an element of coincidence," a historian writes, but "only at the end of that [the nineteenth] century was comfort taken for granted." He goes on to explain, "this expectation was based upon confident belief that within [the new 'White City'] a Comfortable House for all was a realistic goal," and happily he concludes, "To a greater extent than nowadays remembered, that expectation and that goal were realized" within the period he is investigating, 1890-1930. Unfortunately, there is a great deal of evidence to the contrary -- namely, the extensive housing problems in Non-White City that generated, among other efforts, unsuccessful low-income housing programs in the subsequent decades, such as Public Housing, Urban Renewal, Habitat for Humanity.

Another way of saying the Great Plains was a frontier is to say it was a battleground: Europeans against Non-Europeans, for example, or the cattle trade against farming. Clearly, it has remained one despite Turner's announcement in 1893 that battles here were a thing of the past: struggles over natural resources, conflicts over water allocation, disputes over the use of public lands, the ever accelerating war against nature waged by agribusiness. Similarly, another way of saying that the concept of the Comfortable House was triumphant at the beginning of the twentieth century is to say that ideas about house building at that time became familiar, unthreatening, generally conservative. Again, there is evidence that this was not the case:

U.S. Patent No. 430,480 (1890), row housing served by central kitchen.

89

the development of new housing types such as a cooperative, multi-family dwelling or row housing with centralized kitchen facilities. These innovative ideas about housing constituted a battlecry, and it was raised by women who do not seem to have taken anything for granted -- except, perhaps, opposition to the alternatives they were formulating, which Dolores Hayden has identified as a "domestic revolution":

> ... The home will no longer be a Procrustean bed...to which each feminine personality must be made to conform by whatever maiming or fatal, spiritual or intellectual oppression... (1917)

If anything is "not remembered nowadays," it is this battle cry, for it was outshouted by an endless promotional barrage:

> ... A beautifully prepared book of 120 pages that covers every phase of the home building project. Over 100 dwellings and garages are pictured and described... (1920s)

Nevertheless, the struggle of women to break the bonds tying them to the restricted role of housewife/homemaker survived the mail-order house, which ceased to be manufactured in the depression of the 1930s. The struggle against the traditional family structure and its housing types reappeared with the women's liberation movement of the late-twentieth century, which generated, among other innovations, single-parent apartment complexes and various cooperative living arrangements for support groups. The outline of a submerged history, of suppressed housing alternatives, has re-emerged in the Great Plains, as elsewhere, faint but insistent.

"Oh, housing alternatives... that old story... cranks... radicals..."

"Yes, housing alternatives... common interests... community needs..."

The cries mingle and are blown across the vast expanse of the Great Plains. The myths surrounding and the conflicts within the freestanding house are among the region's defining characteristics.

SOURCES (in order of appearance in the essay)

Part 1, Sod House
Dick, Everett. The Sod-House Frontier.
     Lincoln: University of Nebraska
     Press, 1954.
Ruede, Howard. Sod House Days. Edited
     by John Ise. Lawrence: University
     Press of Kansas, 1983.
Welsch, Roger. Sod Walls. Broken Bow,
     Nebraska: Purcells, 1968.

Part 2, Schoolhouse
Cather Willa. "The Best Years," The
     Old Beauty and Others. New York:
     Alfred A. Knopf, 1948.
Fuller, Wayne. One-Room Schools of
     the Middle West. Lawrence:
     University Press of Kansas, 1994.
Benjamin, Walter. "One Way Streets,"
     Reflections. New York: Harcourt
     Brace Jananovich, 1979.
Foucault, Michel. The Archaeology of
     Knowledge. New York: Pantheon
     Books, 1972.
Holl, Steven. Rural and Urban House
     Types of North America. New York:
     Pamphlet Architecture (No. 9), 1982.
Barna, Joel. "Stream and Consciousness,"
     Progressive Architecture, November, 1992.

Part 3, Balloon Frame Construction

Bennett, Mildred. The World of Willa Cather. Lincoln: University of Nebraska Press, 1961.

Lee, Hermione. Willa Cather: Double Lives. New York: Pantheon Books, 1989.

Brown Duncan. Frank Lloyd Wright: Plan Types to 1915. Unpublished Master's dissertation, School of Architecture and Urban Design, University of Kansas.

Peterson, Fred. Homes in the Heartland. Lawrence: University Press of Kansas, 1992.

Stone, Joan. "Dance in Kansas at the Turn of the Century." Unpublished pamphlet used as program for dance, Sweet Home. Lawrence, Kansas: 1987. (Printed.)

Part 4, House as Commodity

Adorno, Theodor. "Popular Music," Introduction to the Sociology of Music. New York: Seabury Press, 1976.

Spencer, Brian (Editor). The Prairie School Tradition. New York: Watson-Guptill Publications, 1979.

Gowans, Alan. The Comfortable House. Cambridge: The MIT Press, 1986.

Hayden, Dolores. The Grand Domestic Revolution. Cambridge: The MIT Press, 1981.

HAMLET,

TOWNSHIP,

INTERIOR

COUNTY

SEAT

EXTERIOR

(1885-86).

North Dakota is the world.
                    Thomas McGrath

PREFACE. The European city as transplanted into America was essentially a coastal city with regional variations: New England, the mid-Atlantic states, the south, along the Gulf of Mexico to the Mississippi delta. The southwest was a special condition, for the European intervention came via Mexico. A second generation and modification of the European city extended these regional variations inland, but principally along waterways such as the Ohio/Mississippi river system. This period of city building lasted about 200 years -- up to the Civil War. What followed in the course of the next 100 years was quite different: the development of a city with distinctly American features, such as streets lined with freestanding, balloon frame houses or steel frame skyscrapers, which took root on the flatlands in the middle portion of the nation. What is most striking about this city of the plains is the divergence from the time-honored notions about urban design European in origin.

After a map of Champlain's settlement on Sainte Croix Island, Maine (1604).

Public Square

State House

Plan of Columbus, Ohio (1817).

97

a leading exponent of "high-tech" design in Europe recently wrote:

Sometimes it is important to find out what a city is -- instead of what it was, or what it should be. That is what drove me to Atlanta -- an intuition that the real city at the end of the 20th century could be found there... [He found that] Atlanta has changed with

Aerial view: what a city is -- (1990) -- not what it was.

unbelievable speed... It reveals some of the most critical shifts in architecture/urbanism of the past 15 years, the most important being the shift from center to periphery and beyond... In fact, Atlanta shifted so completely that the center/edge opposition is no longer the point...

To properly understand this European's perception of "center/edge opposition," which was never "the point" of the American city, a short detour to Europe is called for.

IN THE BEGINNING was the grid -- in the great Plains, of course, but also in Europe as far back as 1100 B.C. A historian writes:

Straight streets meeting at right angles were known in Nebuchadnezzar's Babylon (c. 1126-1105 B.C.). [However,] Aristotle seems to have thought such planning was invented by Hippodamus of Miletus [in the period c. 480 - 350 B.C. In any

98

case,] the preferred Greek method of planning was per stringas -- that is to say, by bands in which east-west avenues were crossed at right angles by one or more north-south streets.

Plan of port of Athens ascribed to Hippodamus.

This reference to cardinal points represents a significant aspect of the application of the grid in planning the city of antiquity. The historian explains:

Such ancient texts as survive on city planning are concerned, not so much with the geometry of streets, as with aspect, prospect, and climate. Hippocrates, for instance, suggests that the healthiest aspect will be facing east, and Aristotle agrees.

As for winds, Vitruvius thought they were represented correctly on the eight-sided Tower of the Winds in Athens "and so, accordingly, should a city be planned," he concluded.

Vitruvius discussed the subjective element in planning, the gridiron form, and made a distinction between "symmetry" and "eurhythmy." The latter term referred to an adjustment of the grid to the "airs, waters, plant life" -- that is the "spirit" of each site. Similarly,

Plan of town in Roman Britain (2nd century A.D.).

99

in the Sophist Plato observed that proportioning was not a matter of plotting a set of rules, but of judging a series of relationships as seen by the eye of an observer.

Urban design in the Middle Ages tends to be associated with winding streets, irregularly shaped open spaces, and picturesque skylines. However, remnants of new towns built in Europe from about 1220 to 1350 and the much-studied plan of the monastery of St. Gall (c. 820-930 A.D.) indicate that the concept of grid survived the fall of Rome with added layers of meaning. The order of the grid in this period is a mirror of an imperial and theocratic society. The laws governing location and orientation within a monastery of church and cloister; quarters for monks (the dorter), novices, guests, pilgrims, and paupers; orchards, gardens, mill and storage facilities; workshops and quarters for craftworkers, artisans, and so on... all reflect laws governing an ordered cosmos as well as an authoritarian regime. Clearly, we are far removed from the real

New town founded by city of Lucca (1255).

church

dorter

latrine

novices

cemetery

Model of St Gall plan.

estate grids of the Great Plains.

If we continue to limit ourselves to cursory historical glimpses of urban grids in Europe, we can look next at a painting by Luciano Laurana (c. 1420-79) in the Ducal Palace at Urbino in central

After a painting by Luciano Laurana.

Italy. Here the grid spreads sidewards from a central axis, but is stopped by the lines of one-point perspective, which force the eye of the observer inward to an eternal, static center. Here the fixed hierarchy of built forms of the heavenly city of the Middle Ages has been translated into the ideal city of the Renaissance.

Baroque urban design, on the other hand, is dynamic. In its play of solid and void, light and dark, with its use of a small trapezoidal space juxtaposed with a large, transverse oval, Bernini's design for the piazza in front of St. Peter's in Rome (1656-66)

Aerial view of St. Peter's piazza.

induces the observer, for the first time in
this survey, to shift positions, to see an

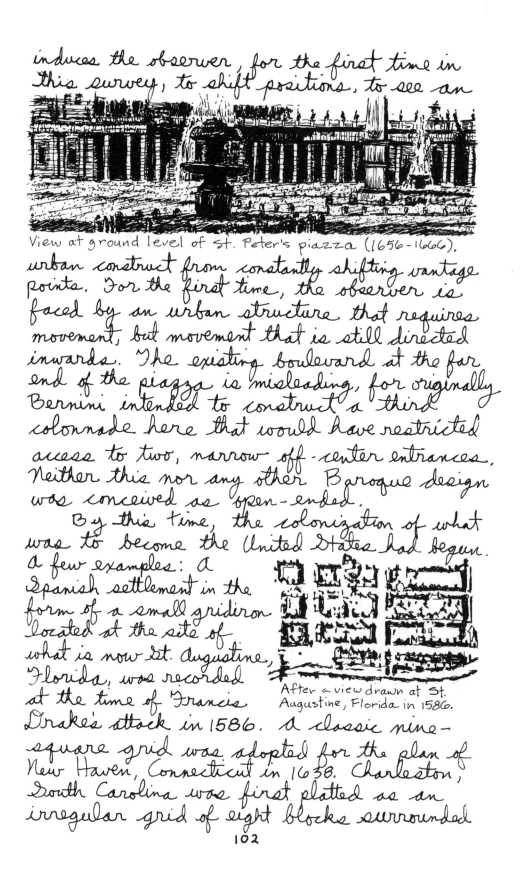

View at ground level of St. Peter's piazza (1656-1666).

urban construct from constantly shifting vantage
points. For the first time, the observer is
faced by an urban structure that requires
movement, but movement that is still directed
inwards. The existing boulevard at the far
end of the piazza is misleading, for originally
Bernini intended to construct a third
colonnade here that would have restricted
access to two, narrow off-center entrances.
Neither this nor any other Baroque design
was conceived as open-ended.

By this time, the colonization of what
was to become the United States had begun.
A few examples: A
Spanish settlement in the
form of a small gridiron
located at the site of
what is now St. Augustine,
Florida, was recorded
at the time of Francis

After a view drawn at St.
Augustine, Florida in 1586.

Drake's attack in 1586. A classic nine-
square grid was adopted for the plan of
New Haven, Connecticut in 1638. Charleston,
South Carolina was first platted as an
irregular grid of eight blocks surrounded

102

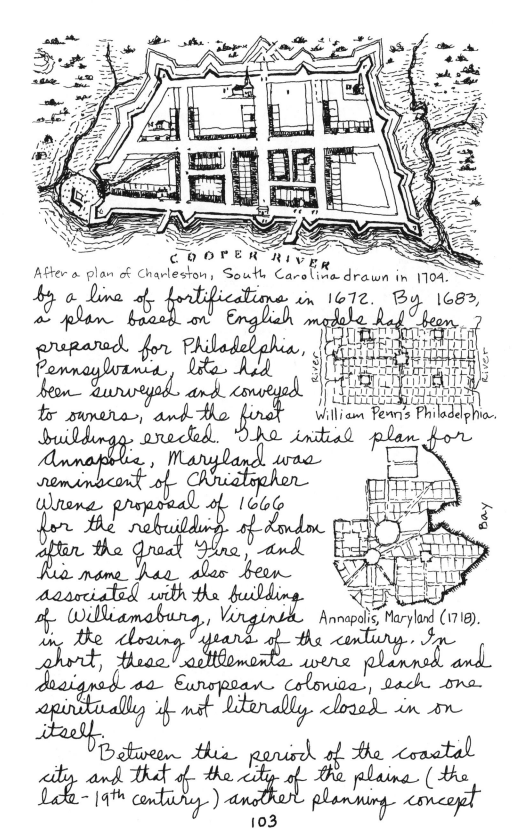

COOPER RIVER

After a plan of Charleston, South Carolina drawn in 1704.

by a line of fortifications in 1672. By 1683, a plan based on English models had been prepared for Philadelphia, Pennsylvania, lots had been surveyed and conveyed to owners, and the first buildings erected. The initial plan for Annapolis, Maryland was reminiscent of Christopher Wrens proposal of 1666 for the rebuilding of London after the great Fire, and his name has also been associated with the building of Williamsburg, Virginia

William Penn's Philadelphia.

Annapolis, Maryland (1718).

in the closing years of the century. In short, these settlements were planned and designed as European colonies, each one spiritually if not literally closed in on itself.

Between this period of the coastal city and that of the city of the plains (the late-19th century) another planning concept

103

developed in Europe that should be considered in the context of this brief survey. The tradition of English empiricism provided the basis for a new theory of landscape planning and design, as exemplified by the garden at Stourhead, Wiltshire (from 1741).

The garden consists of a series of structures that resemble classical temples, a rocky grotto, and similar "follies," grouped about an artificial lake and

View of 3 "follies," designed hillside, constructed lake at Stourhead.

surrounded by "woods" that replicate the composed landscapes of Claude Lorrain's paintings. Each element represents an incident in Virgil's Aeneid and the owner's life. In the words of a philosopher writing at the time, the design offers " a multitude of intentions and plurality of meanings." Nevertheless, to experience the garden fully, the observer must be familiar with the underlying narrative. The various devices of the design were just so many clues with which the observer could read the narrative "the right way." For all of its intentions and multiple meanings, the design is a closed book.

From here to the plan for Washington, D.C. is a short and convenient step with which to conclude our detour. L'Enfant's famous plan of 1791 indicates squares for the 15 states of the union, each embellished with an appropriate "statue, column, obelisk, or similar ornament." A cascade issues from the base of the Capitol, and a "grand avenue," 400 feet wide flanked by gardens, leads from the Capitol to the Potomac. Various monuments are noted, such as an equestrian statue of Washington and a church for "public prayer, thanksgiving, funeral orations, etc." As a historian has noted: "L'Enfant was a product of his age and the instrument through which certain principles of civic design that had been developed in western Europe found expression on the Potomac River."

L'Enfant's plan for Washington, D.C. (1791).

In all the phenomena we have examined so far, I have emphasized the prescriptive nature of the European urban design tradition. The components of the plan for St. Gall are hierarchically composed and direct the observer to a single objective. The components of St. Peter's piazza, on the other hand, are endowed with equal value and dignity, and the observer is assigned a more active role. Yet, the spatial construct

105

expands toward a totality which is fixed and preordained. The observer's sense of freedom of movement is an illusion, an aspect of Bernini's design. Similarly, a visitor to Washington, D.C. is drawn into L'Enfant's concern with axial treatment of building masses and urban spaces, his delight in sweeping diagonals, and his determination to close vistas with significant buildings and monuments. In short, all of these built environments are unquestionably defined and self-contained.

"This is what drove me to Atlanta," the exponent of European high-tech design explains. He sees the ambiguous building conditions within a rapidly expanding metropolitan district as a field of possibilities open to all sorts of operative choices and architectural interpretations. He sees "what the city is -- not what it was"... in Europe. In the great Plains, however, this kind of indeterminate structure not only is but also was -- even before it could be called a city. This structure can be seen as

an expanding series of grids: section, township, range, county. It also can be experienced: movement from home-place outward through township to county seat.

HAMLET

The road system organized and maintained at the county level has generated a pattern of crossroads development that planners term "unincorporated hamlet." The term, however, is hard to pin down; it sometimes applies to a few scattered houses, sometimes to a cluster of nondescript commercial buildings, sometimes to little more than an isolated church and graveyard. Despite its

church,   graveyard,   county road.

vagueness as built form, its regional significance has qualified more than one of these developments for the National Register of Historic Places.

"Modern construction has been minimal," one nomination for the Register notes and reports that although several buildings have been remodeled, their modest massing and scale as well as generous set-back from the intersection have been maintained. The document explains that "trees and grass still dominate the landscape... surrounding land use patterns will be preserved through an agricultural easement." In other words, despite or because of its lack of distinguishing architectural features this crossroads development inspired the writer of the nomination with a sense of place, of organized dispersion. It should go without saying that it would be wrong to refuse a priori its right to registration as a "historic place" simply because it does not recall built forms that existed long ago and far away. Nevertheless, its nomination calls into question any rigid interpretation of the words "historic" and "place." It challenges planning and design standards that have been considered archetypical since the Middle Ages. How, then, is it to be assessed?

    (1) Each detail of the planning and construction of such a crossroads colony calls traditional architectural standards of evaluation into question.

    (2) What matters are the building options that emerge out of a particular conjunction of construction details cut free from previous associations.

    (3) The value of such a conjunction

lies in its freedom from any tie that would presume to determine built form in advance and its consequent freedom to generate new forms. It offers a field of architectural possibilities.

There is a particular crossroads of neglected buildings near the Kansas-Nebraska border where Joan and I tend to stop for a picnic lunch on our way to visit a friend who lives in Lincoln, about a four-hour drive from our home in Lawrence. The architecture is miserly in its simplicity, but it always seems to greet us with a silent deference as we emerge from our car. At first, the

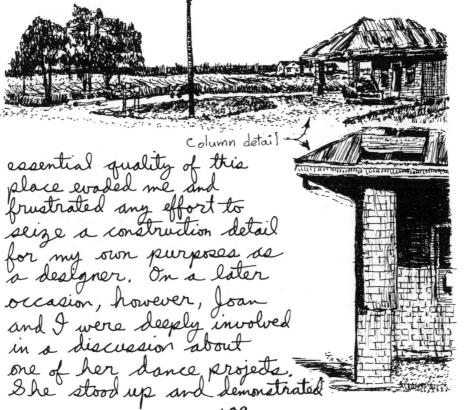

Column detail

essential quality of this place evaded me and frustrated any effort to seize a construction detail for my own purposes as a designer. On a later occasion, however, Joan and I were deeply involved in a discussion about one of her dance projects. She stood up and demonstrated a gesture, and suddenly the place imposed itself on us with all the force of a thing physically experienced. The architectural detail that I had attempted to grasp was, I suddenly realized, indissolubly imbedded within the built form -- that is, the detail and built form were one.

Such is the case with the work of a great architect, such as Louis Kahn's development plan for Philadelphia. His proposal is so transparent, so full of what he was interpreting, that his drawing is a kind of window that opens upon the city William Penn diagrammed. Similarly, the crossroads is a kind of window that opens upon larger, more complex settlement patterns, such as township.

TOWNSHIP AS BUILT FORM. There is no typical example of township. Most of the reasons for diversity rather than typicality spring from the sheer immensity of the Great Plains, extending as it does, from the Rio Grande on the south to the geographically arbitrary Canadian border and roughly 98°-105° meridian east to west. Therefore, there tends to be a diversity of agricultural

activity -- specifically, townships whose principal agricultural activity varies according to differences of climate, water supply, and drainage conditions. This tendency towards specialization has been magnified by the industrialization of farming. For example, one town in western Kansas spreads itself over a vast plain of wheat, while another pulls itself into a collecting point of grain elevators and transportation facilities. Elsewhere, the doors of a township open onto nothing but pastures and transfer pens for cattle.

To this is added a diversity of architectural characteristics that reflect the ethnic, religious, and political identity of those who built these townships. Most of them are noticeably influenced by

111

particular European
building traditions,
while others reflect
Native-American
cultural patterns.
In short, architectural
echoes from around
the world reverberate,
sometimes faintly,
at other times more
insistently, in the
townships of the
great Plains.

Finnish sauna stove built of
rubble and railroad rail.

Another source of diversity can be
traced back to the limitations of
building materials before the advent of the
railways. Because the region was
predominantly composed of tall or
short grassland, an isolated area of
deciduous forest, such as the Black
Hills of South Dakota, or shallow beds
of limestone, such as an area known
for its "post-rock" in northcentral
Kansas, generated local variants of
vernacular building systems. One
example among many is a farmhouse in
post-rock country built of limestone,
but in slabs cut and notched together
as if it were a traditional log structure.
In general, there tend to be two
basic types of rural settlement: one
in which buildings are clustered together,
the other in which they are scattered
and dispersed; but only the latter has

112

taken root in the Plains. There are various forms of dispersion, and again there tend to be two basic types: one consisting of a scatter of institutional and commercial buildings as well as farms, the other corresponding to a scatter of farms around what may be a very rudimentary

spine of institutional and commercial structures, that is, a very modest "Main Street."

The dynamic underlying the first type of dispersed township becomes apparent on a closer look at a particular example in the Red River valley of North Dakota near the Canadian border. A historian of the area explains that in the period from roughly the mid-1870s to mid-1880s, a family named Ethier lived about six miles from an isolated general store owned by a man named Myrick, who presumed he had a monopoly at that site. However, rather than shop at Myrick's store, the Ethiers chose to make an annual trip to Winnipeg, seventy miles away, where they found significantly lower prices. Further, they thought of the trip as a social occasion that more than compensated for any inconvenience it entailed. The historian notes:

What seemed to be a monopoly for Myrick, who had no real competitors at hand and who served a substantial enclave that was separated by many miles from any other, was instead a market in which he had to compete for business. The price he quoted had to be higher because of the freight charges he paid to get goods to his store. The Myrick store was just as isolated as its customers.

The equivalent of a financial analyst of the time concluded that "Myrick's outpost was doing a good business but ought to do better if he did not charge too high prices." One of the reasons the store could "do good business" was that it also could function as a "farmer's P.O." As a fourth-class post office, Myrick's store could keep the box rents it collected and a percentage of postage sales. Further, when people like the Ethiers came by to

INTERIOR

EXTERIOR

114

send off or receive mail, they might engage in what today is called "impulse shopping," buying a food staple or placing an order for some special fabric. Myrick's competitors were not other general stores in open country, but those in a location served by the railroad, Winnipeg, which did not have to bear the expense of overland drayage.

Railroad depot, commercial buildings.

This aspect of Myrick's story suggests the dynamic underlying the formation of the second type of dispersed township. In general, as the variety of goods and services offered in a township increased, so did the number of potential buyers and suppliers. In the Great Plains at this time such a development was likely to increase the interest of the railroad industry, which was laying out new lifelines for the region. The process could be reversed. The very act of a railroad announcing a new line and platting new townsites, or even a rumor of its doing so, could start someone like Myrick thinking. Rather than try to exploit his isolated location, he could try to exploit what the railroad identified as a "market area." He could link up with other stores and shops, a newspaper, a hotel with a professional office or two, and, of course, be near a railroad. Today he might think about getting involved in a "Main Street Program." As it turned out, people like Myrick had little choice in the matter, for the railroad industry was imposing just such a pattern on the entire region.

A hundred years later, the imposition of corporate-style farming on the landscape coupled with the development of farm machinery that can pay for itself only if operated over an extensive area are creating a form of township dispersion so extreme that terms like "home-place," "Main Street," even "market area," as geographic entities, take on nostalgic overtones. That is what is happening in those parts of the Great Plains being reshaped by center-pivot, deep-well irrigating systems, such as those defined by the Ogallala aquifer, which extends from southern Texas through western Oklahoma and Kansas into Nebraska. The rural base is being revolutionized: gone is a variety of crops, monoculture has taken its place; gone, too, is the image of the "family farm" and a significant number of agricultural workers. The built form of township, its network of relationships, is being reshaped, breaking certain linkages in the process and placing the whole under severe stress. A larger schema, but one not unlike the old, is settling into place.

The diversity of township as built form can thus be traced to irregularities, technological developments, and to the history of the region before as well as after passage of the Homestead Act in 1862. Its geometry can be traced back to the Land Ordinance of 1785; its openness, to Native American patterns of adaptation to the environment. The patterns are super-imposed upon one another: a tensile web upon a compressive grid upon meandering trails. Each pattern has endured,

First townships surveyed (1786), each is 6 square miles, 36 square sections.

accommodating change and modifications to do so, each affecting and being affected by the others. This adaptability and openness can be viewed as a strength of township as built form -- or weakness, depending on the observer's point of view and what an observer is looking for. Thinking in the romantic terms of the "open road," one observer sees just that. Thinking in the picturesque terms of "townscape," another observer sees nothing but endless fields, an occasional farm complex, a road inter-section with a convenience store and gas pumps, fencing that consists of a few strands of barbed wire, a line of trees -- in short, nothing of architectural value.

TOWNSHIP AS MODEL can be seen as a web of relationships radiating outward from home-place. The proprietor of the general store had a pivotal position in this radiating web as a key source of information. A merchant traveling in the region in the 1870s explained, "For my purposes, I

regard a general store as the civic center of the countryside. A notary knows far less than a store's proprietor about what goes on in a small place. Here is a fellow merchant, an organizer of special events, a creditor and sometimes usurer." The general store rivaled the churches as a meeting place, for it was a clearing house of political ideas and current fashions. "The radiating web of relationships was reinforced by people helping one another to raise someone's barn or build a schoolhouse; to deal with a mutual problem, such as a fire or plague of grasshoppers, or civic improvement, such as a modest library.

This set of relationships overlapped with others: one township had an inviting, spring-fed creek and a sulfur spring; a second, a source of stone; another,

sulfur creek tour boat (ca. 1900).

119

a popular fairground and festival; and so on. This could generate a sense of rivalry among townships and feuds that ended in long drawn-out lawsuits, especially concerning property rights of scarce water resources. Ideological differences could also generate hostility between townships: this one was settled by abolitionists, that one was pro-slavery; one township was founded as a religious commune, another developed as a trailhead that catered to the needs of transient cattle drivers. There could also be fierce quarrels over prestige: which township carried away the best prizes from the annual fair; which had the biggest... the tallest...

Births, baptisms, weddings, funerals, holidays, special events, such as a Camp Meeting or Chautauqua, could get people travelling from one township to another. There was also the need to

Communal baptism in township pond.

move things. During breaks in the agricultural cycle, a farmer might "hitch-up the team" as a way to earn some extra money or simply help a friend in a nearby community.

The distinctive character of the Great Plains model becomes apparent when it is compared with an equivalent model on

120

Courthouse ← Schoolhouse

the Atlantic seaboard or in the Ohio and Mississippi river valleys at a similar stage of development. A historian notes:

> Treatment of the green or public square received the greatest attention from the planners of the Reserve's communities [in Ohio]. The rectangle at Sharon Center, the ellipse at Leroy, the parallelogram at Madison... may simply have resulted from imitations of the home communities of the planners in New England... [or] efforts to experiment with different forms in search for a better plan...

In either case, traditional notions of European town planning were being employed. In contrast, the great Plains township as a model cannot be recorded or manipulated in the form of a geometric diagram. It materializes only to the extent that it is a site of a succession of transformations.

COUNTY SEAT. Between the mid-19th and mid-20th centuries the county seat was the place rural life came into contact with the outside world: trade, administration, justice. It is the place someone went to find a notary, lawyer, or justice of the peace, the tax collector and the law. It was also the place someone went to find a pharmacist or a doctor, or someone with special skills, such as a gun-smith, and a place to find special foods, such as sausages, hams, and sweets. Only a tiny volume of goods made its way into rural life through this channel; nevertheless, it represented

County Courthouse interior.

a link to the outside world and as such stimulated and enlivened the surrounding area.

There also were special building types in a county seat, such as the courthouse and jail or railroad station and a hotel that accommodated commercial travellers and activities frowned upon in the churches. Another way the meaning of the county seat can be seen is by looking more closely at one of these buildings. A description of a hotel in Dakota Territory during the 1880s

122

pictures a crude wooden structure. A
guest pushes open a flimsy door with an
equally flimsy "catch" and enters a dingy
cubicle separated from the adjacent
cubicle by a sheet of brown building
paper. The dim light shed by a
smoky kerosene lamp reveals a wobbly
bed with a hay-filled pillow and a
wash stand with a crude bowl and
pitcher containing suspicious-looking
water. The harsh sound of a gong
announces dinner. The guest hurries
to the dining room but realizes that
there is time to use the wash room,
which is located at one side of the
room.

"This won't do! Landlord, look at
this towel!"

That worthy with an air of innocent
surprise exclaims, "There's 26 people.

used that towel before you and you're the first to complain. I sure hope you can put up with our fare which is darned hard."

It turns out to be stale bread, rancid bacon, very black coffee, and a wooden toothpick. After supper, the guest picks up the cigar that also came with the meal and moves towards the bar at the far end of the room. Having "liquored up a bit," a group has gathered around the stove for an evening of conversation and stories, but the guest decides against joining in order to write a letter instead.

The hotel dining room has now become a bar room, a smoking room for the group by the stove, a writing room for the guest, a reading room for some, and a whittling room or just plain standing-around room for others. It is the largest room in the settlement for important meetings and political debates. People in Elwood, Kansas are pleased to relate that Abraham Lincoln delivered an address in their hotel dining room in 1860 and then "spun a few yarns by the glowing stove." During the summer, much of this activity moves outdoors onto the hotel veranda or into the adjacent field, where our guest might see the elaborate wagon of an itinerant huckster as well

124

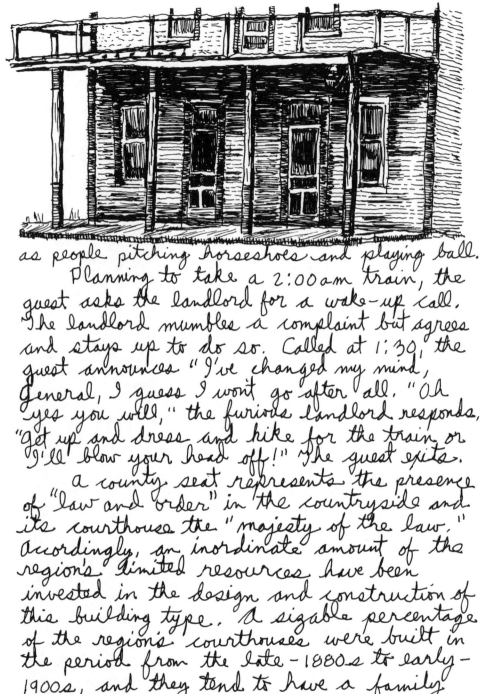

as people pitching horseshoes and playing ball.

Planning to take a 2:00 am train, the guest asks the landlord for a wake-up call. The landlord mumbles a complaint but agrees and stays up to do so. Called at 1:30, the guest announces "I've changed my mind, General, I guess I won't go after all." "Oh yes you will," the furious landlord responds, "get up and dress and hike for the train or I'll blow your head off!" The guest exits.

A county seat represents the presence of "law and order" in the countryside and its courthouse the "majesty of the law." Accordingly, an inordinate amount of the region's limited resources have been invested in the design and construction of this building type. A sizable percentage of the region's courthouses were built in the period from the late-1880s to early-1900s, and they tend to have a family resemblance to one another or, rather, a common architectural influence, namely the work of H. H. Richardson (1838-1886). These courthouses can be recognized by their massive silhouettes, heavy towers, and yawning archways; their great blocks of granite, sandstone, or limestone (never marble); their bold stone carving, thick textures, deep colors... all characteristics of Richardson's work.

What accounts for this attraction of Richardson's architecture to people in the Great Plains at this particular time? Perhaps economic and social conditions have something to do with it. As it turns out, the profits to be made from securing the location of a county seat at this time were substantial. According to a historian of the region, if all went well, the founders could secure over $500,000 for a staked area that cost them something in the nature of $3,000 – $4,000. This was enough fuel to ignite "county-seat wars in the vast majority of counties in Kansas, Nebraska, and the Dakotas." The historian explains that some of these disputes were settled at the ballot box, but others led to "interminable quarrels, bloodshed, and

(1885-86).

126

loss of life." County-seat wars differed, but they had certain characteristics in common: "a disdain for truth, a complete lack of honor, a willingness to adopt any corrupt practice..." all in order to beat the competition. In such an atmosphere, a Richardsonian courthouse might appear to have the attributes of a fortress and radiate a sense of security.

Nevertheless, whatever strength these courthouses may have seemed to possess was skin deep, even if that skin was a thick assortment of Richardsonian motifs. The same economic and social forces that created the county seat also defeated the Richardsonian facade. Concerning the design of a courthouse in Texas (1890-91), an architectural historian observes that, "in spite of their massive voussoirs and rusticated masonry, the walls appear thin and two-dimensional and the water table too weak to support the superstructure." The author also notes similar subversive tendencies, such as "insistent verticality in several

(1891-93),

127

other of the Texas excursions into Richardsonian Romanesque."

Whatever "majesty" the Richardsonian facade possessed was also skin deep. A description of an election held in this period indicates something about the people who made their way into these buildings:

About nine o'clock the judges arrived and one notary public to swear them in. A McQuinn and two McArtles were the judges. One of them could not write his name and had to mark in signing his affidavit. The notary public and the old man McArtle were appointed clerks of Election. One of these numbers had to have a deputy write for him, and still he had to keep the poll list...

Another description, this time of a political meeting, is even more revealing:

The meeting has just begun but the air is already blue with cigar smoke and people can scarcely see across the room... The candidates jump onto the platform and desks, bellowing slogans at each other and the room at large... They have a full supply of agrarian grievances at their disposal; free and unlimited coinage of silver... restrict foreclosures... temperance

These issues generated another force that battered against the stolid Richardsonian facade: the Farmer's Alliance and the People's Party, the tumultuous rise and precipitous fall of Populism in the final decades of the century.

128

THE OUTLINE OF A MODEL for the development of built forms of the great Plains can be seen by shifting our focus away from isolated details. We can see this model breaking up and dispersing what architects and planners tend to honor as "town center," and see the extension of this phenomenon into what they disparage as "edge cities." The model is presented in a favorable light in Frank Lloyd Wright's description of "Broadacre City" and the European architect's observations concerning Atlanta with which this discussion began.

In an effort to define the model, I shall begin with a passage written in 1868 by Frederick Law Olmsted concerning a project near Chicago that he was working on at the time and try to indicate the nature of its relationship to the current scene:

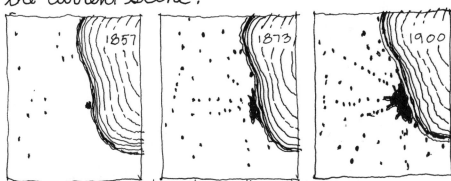

Chicago settlement and growth pattern.

"It would appear that the demands of suburban life, with reference to civilized refinement, are not a retrogression from, but an advance upon, those which are characteristic of town life, and that no great town can long exist without great suburbs."

129

"It would appear that the   "suburban sprawl"
demands of suburban life..."

Nowadays, the term, "suburban life," refers to a general aspect of our culture that has been the object of numerous planning studies. Many of these have been devoted to a "problem of suburban sprawl" determined by an extensive amount of natural environment lost coupled with a correspondingly limited amount of built environment gained. Some of these studies have been quite insightful, but the body of work has not constituted a significant challenge to assumptions about the European city nor to principles and precepts of urban design based upon them. A good deal of attention has also been given to forms of social relationship and communication in the suburbs involving a large number of people invariably identified as "middle class". It has been explained how these forms of social interaction are, paradoxically, in total contrast to any idea of collectivity and, as such, harbingers of "the death of public life."

"It would appear that the demands of suburban life, with reference to civilized refinement..."

130

It goes without saying that neither planners nor architects would use such a politically charged term as "civilized refinement" these days, but it is precisely this notion that inspires their futile attempts to recreate spanish "plazas," French "boulevards," and English residential "crescents" and "squares" in American cities. An article written in 1995 explains:

Plan. Model.

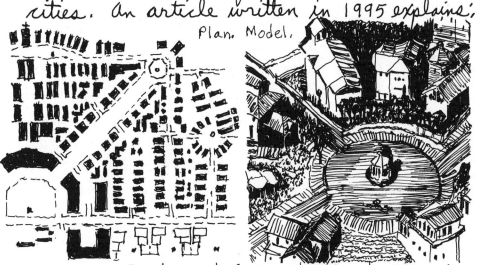

The highly publicized project of Seaside, Florida (1980s).

Over the past several years, urban designers have made a remarkably concerted movement toward healing their breach with the past. What comes through in [their promotional materials] these days is a desire to apply to today's circumstances, the traditional urban framework of streets, squares, and pedestrian scale spaces [with nostalgic labels such as "village green"].

In short, what comes through are vague notions about "civilized refinement."

"It would appear the demands of suburban life, with reference to civilized refinement, are not

131

a retrogression from, but an advance upon, those which are characteristic of town life..."

Today, the notion of going "into town" in order to work, shop, or attend a cultural event and returning to a "cozy home in suburbia" is archaic. Standardization and eternal expansion of the city have combined to produce built environments, which as one observer has written...

look not at all like our old cities. Buildings rarely rise shoulder to shoulder, as in Chicago's Loop. Instead, their broad, low outlines dot the landscape like mushrooms, separated by greensward and parking lots... There are jogging trails... [Districts are not] tied together by locomotives and subways, but by jetways, freeways, and rooftop satellite dishes... Their characteristic monument is not a horse-mounted hero, but atria reaching for the sun and shielding trees perpetually in leaf at the cores of corporate head-quarters, fitness centers, and shopping malls.

This pattern constitutes a significant challenge to assumptions about civilized refinement based on a European model, as well as principles and precepts of urban

132

design based upon them. Olmsted's concluding thought -- "no great town can long exist without great suburbs" -- should be read in the light of this development.

Study of additions to Jefferson's design for the Virginia State Capitol (after Leon Krier, 1982).

My critical eye has before it the insistent challenge of a settlement pattern for which there is no equivalent in Europe. Does this mean that there is no room in this built form for the breadth of interpretation of an urban designer such as Louis Kahn or Leon Krier? Since the ever-expanding pattern of dispersion could theoretically encompass the industrialized world, is there any guarantee that it will not then lapse into architectural babel as did the biblical structure? The first question concerns the elementary conditions necessary for a Louis Kahn or Leon Krier to recognize potentially richer, deeper meanings within a settlement pattern. The second presumes that, in order to articulate an implicit vision of the built environment and its relationship with a variety of cultures,

133

a settlement pattern must at least have the requisites of that architectural discourse known as "urban design."

From a cultural viewpoint, the city of the plains calls into question univocal relationships as well as the notion of center/edge opposition previously noted. This is inherent in the pattern, for its outward thrust is culturally charged, primed by sociological shifts, and activated by technological developments. The European city may be viewed as a progression from the classical geometric forms of the Renaissance city to the non-Euclidian geometries of the industrialized city. On the other hand, the city of the plains may be viewed as a progression from abstract forms to forms that are nonfinite. The city of the plains does not cause a break with Cartesian rationalism, it is the break. What possibilities does it offer an urban designer?

The more dispersed and loosely organized a settlement pattern is, the greater is its potential as an origin of possible metropolitan structures. Only certain settlement patterns have to be understood univocally with no possibility for misunderstanding or individual interpretation. "The Forbidden City" of Peking and Versailles during the reign of Louis XIV are two well known examples. Other settlement patterns convey an abundance

134

Versailles seen from the air.

of possible meanings, as is the case with contemporary Beijing or Paris, for example. A classical city, such as Washington, D.C., avails itself of a few deviations from certain design conventions, such as the intrusion of the Smithsonian Building into the Mall, only to reendorse them later, as demonstrated by the museum's later additions. Whereas, a sprawling city calls those conventions into question even as it uses them for its own subversive ends. It presents a web of suggestions, as opposed to cross-axes of symmetrically disposed statements. Its value to an urban designer hinges precisely on the ambiguity of these suggestions, for they can lead a designer far beyond the confines of the geometric diagrams delineated by a L'Enfant or William Penn. To describe the city of the plains more precisely, to define it more accurately, a closer look at a particular feature, Main Street, is called for.

SOURCES

Broadbent, Geoffrey. Emerging Concepts in
 Urban Space Design. London: Van Nostrand
 Reinhold (International), 1990.

Braudel, Fernand. The Identity of France. New
 York: Harper and Row, 1990.

Dick, Everett. The Sod-House Frontier. Lincoln:
 University of Nebraska Press, 1979.

Eco, Umberto. The Open Work. Cambridge:
 Harvard University Press, 1989.

Fein, Albert. Frederick Law Olmsted and the
 American Environmental Tradition. New York:
 George Braziller, 1972.

Garreau, Joel. Edge City. New York: Doubleday, 1988.

Hudson, John. Plains Country Towns. Minneapolis:
 University of Minnesota Press, 1985.

Koolhaas, Rem. "Atlanta", Progressive Architecture
 (November, 1994).

Langdon, Philip. "Learning from the Traditional
 City." Progressive Architecture (January, 1995).

Larson, P. & Brown, S. (eds.) The Spirit of H. H.
 Richardson on the Midland Prairies. Ames: Iowa
 State University Press, 1990.

Reps, John. The Making of Urban America. Princeton:
 Princeton University Press, 1965.

MAIN STREET: DOWN BY THE RIVER,

THE RAILROAD COMES TO TOWN,

THE AUTOMOBILE TAKES COMMAND,

AIRPORT SHUTTLE

Perceived as a ribbon of unfolding possibilities, Main Street represented a rejection of the classical notion of street as an axis of symmetrical planning but not a rejection of the notion of street as an urban corridor with defining walls. It did not represent the death of the built form; rather it proposed a new, more flexible version of it. The disorder of its commercial signs, the randomness of its skyline, the explosion of architectural styles incited people to make their own connections.

QUESTION: How in each period of the development of the Great Plains were various building systems and design currents developed and dispersed? Why in the process of dispersion did they fracture along certain lines and in certain directions? How have they been elaborated and transformed over time? These questions should be considered in the context of the larger history of the region, for it is this history which reveals the collective effort that goes into these systems and currents of thought. It is this history which indicates how the building activity of each period subsumes and absorbs all previous building activity, including all of its mistakes and follies, successes and dreams. From the earliest days of a city located on the

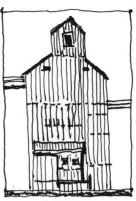

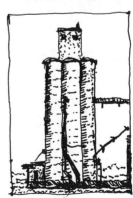

139

Missouri River, Main Street has played a major role. There is, of course, no such thing as the true story of Main Street nor anything like a true story. The following attempt to identify a few of the story's vital, if disconnected, facts and to pick up some of the threads of their relationships can, at best, suggest the direction of the story's development, its historical trajectory.

DOWN BY THE RIVER. The story of this particular Main Street begins in the mid-1820s, when a flood forced the relocation of a few log cabins built by fur traders a few miles upstream from their original location near the confluence of the Missouri and one of its tributaries. Within the next ten years two towns were created within a few miles of the relocated trading post, towns that became established staging and outfitting centers for wagons headed west. In the mid-1840s, Main Street was cut through the bluffs in the vicinity of the old trading post, connecting the area's first road system with the river and establishing what would

140

become an ever-expanding pattern of regional relationships. The development sequence began as a clear and logical relationship between the river system and an embryonic web of regional roads radiating from "Main Street," which was simply an extension of a wharf constructed at the river edge. At that time, the wharf consisted of a cluster of a few stores, workshops, and houses where business between a town merchant and the passing steamboat was conducted. Until 1850

merchants felt it best to cling to the wharf in locating a business; even the town newspaper and doctor were located in a building facing it.

Main Street was unpaved. During rainy weather wooden planks were laid across the intersections to help pedestrians trying to cross what often became a river of mud in which abandoned wagons were hopelessly mired down. A popular joke of the time relates the story of someone who seeing a hat on the roadway, gets off his horse to pick it up. "Imagine his surprise

to find it on the head of a woman who
explained she was on a wagon and safe
enough, but she supposed her horses and
wagon were in a mighty bad fix." When
the roadway was dry, galloping horses
and lumbering wagons kicked up dust
that hot summer winds blew through open
windows onto everything and everyone. A
mixture of wood frame and brick buildings,
one to three stories
high, flanked the
street with a random
assortment of facades,
wooden sidewalks,
and disconnected
wooden awnings.
What was missing,
in comparison with
the design associated with a European city,
was a tonal center that would allow an
observer to predict the development of the
city plan or its architecture. The progression
from one architectural style and building
type to another was arbitrary. Considered
in terms of the most elementary European
settlement pattern, the links of this relational
network had no privileged direction. That
lack can now be seen to have been a
positive aspect of the evolution of an
American city with its own characteristics.
     Main Street was extended several
blocks in from the river during a boom
period of the 1850s. There were painted
signs that one might expect to see: billiard

142

parlor and saloon, boots and saddlery, but also signs that identified millinery and furniture shops and a business college. The opening of a wholesale grocery store on the wharf indicated a developing market for local produce. There were the false fronts and irregular line of chopped-off cornices that Hollywood and Disneyland have made familiar, but also masonry arches, classical moldings, intricate ironwork, even a mansard roof.

The building boom of the 1850s began slowly, but with the success of a new four-story, block-long building with stores and offices on the first and second floors respectively, and hotel rooms on the third and fourth, other building activity soon followed. A literary society took over the second floor of one new building; Odd Fellows and Sons of Temperance, that of another; a mixture of lawyers, physicians, insurance agents, and other professionals quickly filled the remaining second-floor space. A series of luxury and specialty retail merchants set up shop, creating a "Shoppers' Promenade" that featured a shop with iron-goods "of the highest quality."

. This growth drove up the cost of land and rentals near the wharf. Development extended down Main Street and adjacent cross streets, merchants moved, wholesale warehousing took over the vacated upper floor space on the wharf, and the area began developing into a wholesaling district. A coffee house became a meeting house for lawyers and their

mercantile and steamboat clients; the back of a cigar shop, a place where vagabonds and river boat workers traded stories; a row of small wooden structures on the wharf contained shops geared to the needs of travelers. At the same time, the mid-1850s, a developer demolished a row of small wooden structures on Main Street to build a brick structure that soon housed a combination exhibition-meeting hall above shops that included a bookstore, an "Emporium of Fashion," and a music store. Most of the merchants who moved into the new building came not from the wharf but from other locations on Main Street itself,

144

This may be explained in part by a decline in the number of travelers and steamboat personnel coming into town; more significantly, it suggests a mood of economic sluggishness on Main Street. A new bakery opened in 1852 but failed three years later, and the owner of the "Emporium of Fashion" fell way behind in his "payments." Indeed, more than half the businesses in the older portion of Main Street were in financial trouble in 1856. Even a budget "one price store," whose entry onto the scene indicated economic decline, closed its doors. Given the number of wooden structures and generally poor quality of their construction, fires were inevitable. What is more significant is how

the business community responded to them. In a boom period the charred ruins tended to be replaced with block-long, mixed-use developments faced with brick. In the mid-1850s, however, few of the burned-out businesses reopened, and those that did were "just getting along." The fact that only half of the stores were insured is another indication of poor business conditions. It is not surprising, then, to note a "crash" in 1857 with an accompanying decrease in business activity and real estate values on Main Street.

During these first decades of the city's history, its economy was controlled by a small oligarchy of early settlers. In 1850 the ten richest of them controlled nearly half of the town's wealth, and the two richest owned a quarter of its real estate. One of these was friendly with the owners of the town's first bank. With his financial support the bank was able to survive the crash of 1857 and extend its operations in the following year with a questionable currency-issuing scheme. He soon lost confidence in this dubious venture, however, and withdrew his support. Without it, the bank failed. He repossessed it along with his friends' homes in 1859 and emerged from the disaster with greater control of local affairs. For example, he chose sites for a new post office, two of the town's churches, and its first schools. He initiated projects

Mansion built in 1858.

to improve the town's infrastructure (at nominal personal expense) and, at the same time, was involved in the construction and leasing of housing and commercial projects adjacent to these "civic improvements." In a similar manner and despite the fact that he had built the wharf and the first hotel adjacent to it and provided loans to the first wholesaling merchants on the wharf he did not hesitate to join forces with the railroads that fatally undermined the steamboat system. When ground was broken for the first rail line, it was he who "performed the honors."

Railway depot built in 1867.

THE RAILROAD COMES TO TOWN.

The area where this city was located had a population of about 4,500 in 1860, only 3,500 at the end of the Civil War, but numbered something like 20,000 people by 1867. In 1865 the first railroad line reached the levee and by 1869 the Missouri River had been bridged, providing connections with a second line. While river traffic was being replaced by rail,

147

Main Street itself began to replace the wharf as the focus of the region's business activity. In the 1870's the city developed as a distribution center. Stockyards, meat packing plants, grain elevators, and flour mills were built in a low lying peninsula of land formed by the looping course of the river, which was referred to as "the Bottoms." Significantly, it was not connected with the river, but to rail facilities that were built at the same time together with the depot that soon became "a scene of more activity than previously found in the mercantile stores, livery stables, the courthouse, and print shop combined." According to the descendant of the owner of the newspaper, its reporters "haunted the depot as a major source of information, interviewing travelers who were a source of news and gossip from the outside world."

A retired depot agent explained, "If a business wanted anything from the outside world or sent to it, it had to deal with me directly or indirectly." The vital role of the community the depot played in the life continued to increase as the region's population grew and its railroad network expanded.

Meanwhile, Main Street was becoming an ever more diverse mixture of activities, building types, and oddly juxtaposed styles. At Second Street (a numbering system that began at the wharf and survived its disappearance) a hotel, whose Second Empire styling was supposed to make it the most fashionable building in the city, failed, was bought by the county, and converted into a courthouse. At Fifth

County Courthouse, converted hotel.

Street wagons filled the public square to the north of city hall on market days, transforming it into a produce market that over time was to take over the entire area. A lumbering parade of weighty commercial buildings that had begun at Sixth Street and in 1872 was approaching Tenth Street was brought to an abrupt halt by the "Panic of 1873." In this decade the population increased to 60,000; the town leaders built more public schools; organized fire and police departments; introduced street lights and horse-drawn streetcars, a building code and a new city charter; constructed a waterworks; and instituted the first of a series of land annexations that were periodically to extend the city south and east.

Even a notion of city building that values economic vitality, freedom of action, and unregulated growth rests on a dialectic between built forms and social relationships. Main Street could continue to develop as such only if it rested on this base; beyond a certain point of imbalance, it would become merely a commercial strip. To establish the required balance the builders of Main Street had to organize technological developments, especially transportation linkages, while at the same time defining the street as an unfolding ribbon of relationships.

After the Panic of 1873, which in fact lasted until the end of the decade, rapid settlement of the upper Great Plains in the 1880s was facilitated by a decade in which sufficient rain fell each year to grow grain even in the normally arid portions of the region. This period of prosperity was reflected in

Catholic Church (1874-75).

150

the rhythm of construction on Main Street, but this boom collapsed in 1888. A march of commercial buildings has continued down Main Street in a cycle of booms and busts to the present day. In the decade of the 1880s the city's population increased from less than 60,000 to over 125,000. In 1886 an electric power company was organized and a cable car system began to replace the horse-drawn streetcars. A new charter in 1889 changed, among other things, the community's name from Town to City, and in 1891 a massive new city hall was built.

Perceived as an unfolding ribbon of possibilities, Main Street represented a rejection of the classical notion of street as an axis of symmetrical planning but not a rejection of the notion of street as an urban corridor with defining walls. It did not represent the death of the traditional built form; rather it proposed a new, more flexible version of it. The disorder of its commercial signs, the randomness of its skyline, the explosion of architectural styles incited people to make their own connections. But the street itself existed in time and space, and it led people further and further away from the river. The area adjacent to the wharf now functioned solely as a wholesale food market, and agriculture continued to dominate the economy. Appropriately, the city's most notable design achievement has been its extensive park and boulevard system, which was largely designed and built in the 1890s.

The design of the park system signalled a shift of the focus of city life and that of Main Street to the south. In 1906 the corner of what is now 23rd and Main was chosen to be the site of a new railway station, and upon completion in 1914, the monumental structure began to have consider-able impact on the

Boulevards and Parks

1893

development pattern of this area. In 1915 the hill to the south of the station, which rose some one hundred feet above street level, was cut through for an extension of Main Street; to the north, Main Street bridged over a maze of railroad tracks to a rapidly developing district of manufacturing and warehousing. In

152

1911 a combination of railroad and agribusiness interests built a second bridge
across the Missouri to an area they
developed into a bleak, smoke-shrouded
industrial wasteland, outside the
jurisdiction of the city's health, sanitary,
fire, safety, and building ordinances,
which sealed the fate of the site of the
original settlement. This generation of
Main street builders wrote off much of
the work of their grandparents in the
name of Big Business; their grandchildren
were to erase the last traces of it in the
name of Urban Renewal.

Growth and another annexation to
the South in 1909 increased the
population from about 160,000 in 1900 to
nearly 250,000 in 1910. Sections of the
park system in the area of the Main Street
extension south of the new railroad station
were completed; one to the southwest in 1904,
another to the east that wrapped around a
new general hospital in 1911. Trolley cars
replaced cable cars, and the system

was extended. But by 1913 the privately owned automobile was already affecting the pattern of urban development.

THE AUTOMOBILE TAKES COMMAND.

For the remainder of the century the relationship of the automobile to traditional notions about urban design was to become a source of increasing anxiety to urban designers, planners, and historians. Although like most americans they were excited by the possibilities offered by this technological development, they felt that it threatened the European paradigms upon which much of their professional work was based. At the same time they had to accommodate the automobile; they had to know what it allowed them to do, what they wanted from it. The automobile forced them to make the latent structure of Main Street manifest.

154

In 1912 Main street in the area of what is now 47th Street was a narrow unpaved lane. However, 60 acres of this low-lying, marshy land had recently been assembled for a project that was to have a profound impact not only on this city but on cities across the nation: a planned shopping district oriented to the suburbs, designed as a "charming village" with decorative stucco wall surfaces, terra cotta and tile ornaments, wrought iron

balconies, tile roofs with picturesque silhouettes, and above all else, an ample amount of free, off-street parking, filling stations, and auto repair facilities, opened for business in the early 1920s. The shoppers' promenade of the 1850's was updated to become a shopping center oriented to the automobile. This development represented more of a modification of the built form of the city of the plains than the introduction of a new settlement pattern, for even as the rate of urbanization had been accelerating in the course of the second half of the 19th century, so too had the rate of suburbanization. First a mud road pushed its way inland from the levee; then the railroad, cable car, and electric trolley generated residential and commercial districts; now the automobile was doing much the same thing. What was only a modifying influence on the built form of the city of the plains was perceived and treated as a corrosive element by urban planners and designers who tried to neutralize the effects of the automobile with antidotes, such as the insertion of subways and elevated rail lines where and when possible.

In the decade of the 1920s ornately decorated movie palaces were built on Main Street, and on top of the hill facing the new rail-road station an extravagant war memorial was erected. A planning commission was initiated, a new city charter written, zoning laws were passed, and a wave of political

war memorial (1923-36).

corruption swept through city hall, depositing a political "boss" and his "machine." Prohibition and gangsters were doing well, and jazz musicians were developing a new art form in clubs hidden away

156

here and there in the alleys behind Main Street. The city continued to grow and by 1930 had a population of nearly 400,000.

Dust bowl years, the depression, 1939: The era of boss rule ended in the penitentiary. World War II: The city's new upper and middle income housing was built in the suburbs while low income housing was confined to the industrial areas of the older city. 1947: a portion of Main Street was included in an area designated as a "central business district," cut off from the adjacent areas by a ring of limited-access trafficways linked to a new interstate highway system.

By 1970 the city had sprawled over 300 square miles and had a population of about a million and a quarter people, less than half of whom lived in the central city. The automobile had replaced the streetcar system, which was terminated in

1957. An international airport was built far to the north of Main Street, transforming the recently prized railroad station into an economic relic. High-rise office buildings were erected on the blocks of Main Street within the area that had been designated the central business district. In the blocks of Main from 46th to 48th Streets, the highly successful shopping district was expanded and its shops became more "exclusive." The district was now the most densely populated area of the region.

In the blocks of Main from 24th to 27th Streets, adjacent to the 1912 extension of Main Street south of the now abandoned railroad station, the first buildings were erected of a privately financed project that in ten years would include some two million square feet of largely speculative office space, low and high-rise condominiums, two luxury hotels, and a 5,000 car parking garage attached to an appropriately scaled "shopper's paradise." A closer look at the design of this garage/paradise feature is revealing.

Truth as regards the order of urban growth or the construction of a wall is of no value here. It is even mandatory to misrepresent and repress certain facts espe-

cially those that per-
tain to building tech-
nology, such as "ma-
sonry" which is plas-
tic and "gas lights"
that are electrified.
Further, the consumer
is asked to accept
architectural discon-
tinuity between the
unrelentingly effi-
cient parking struc-
ture and "exclusive" shops, which resemble toys

lined up on make-believe streets stacked around
a bank of escalators located in an "atrium"
selling "food specialties from around the world."
It seems as if a child's whim has brought it
all together and at any moment might kick
any one or all of the shops away. Architectural
"style" attempts to elicit a favorable response
from the consumer -- in a word, to sell itself.
The architecture does not evoke an abstract

idea of beauty, nor
does style turn in-
to a pretext for for-
mal digressions. It
sells itself to such
an extent that con-
sumers end up de-
siring it. The moment
the design moves to
parking structure,
however, it abandons
any sense of play-

fulness and ventures into the realm of transportation planning in its most mundane form. Horizontal and vertical surfaces are raw concrete, paint
is applied only to mark car locations, "non-slip"
textures are used only where necessary as a
legal precaution, every feature vibrates in the
harsh glare of industrial lighting. Nevertheless,
both client and consumer are satisfied: con-
sumers "enjoy as they buy," and they do it
efficiently.

A historical
style, such as that
of the Italian ren-
aissance, or its de-
velopment by an
architect, such as
Palladio, may have
been unknown to
the builders of
Main Street and
had no direct in-
fluence on the sty-
listic elaborations of their buildings, but this
does not mean the design of Main Street was
not influenced by architectural history. The
builders of Main Street may not have known
the origin of the arch-lintel combination
known as the Palladian motif, but it makes
its appearance in both the older and newer
"street" facades within the shopping mall. In
analyzing the various relationships between
these ingratiating facades to the underlying
structures of the street, formalist criteria
that tend to make distinctions between archi-

160

tectural "kitsch" and "authentic" architecture must be avoided, for this false polarization distorts opposing principles and turns a blind eye to a dialectic between architecture that aims at producing something new and another kind that aims at recalling something old. In this dialectic it is the latter that fulfills the fundamental conditions of establishing acquired design procedures, which Thomas Jefferson, for one, profoundly understood. Because of his keen awareness of the symbolic function of architecture, Jefferson provided a selection of Roman and Palladian orders in his design for the University of Virginia (1817-26). "It is this which gives the main lawn at the University its pervasive archaeological flavor," a historian notes.

Within the architectural situation of Main Street anything is possible. The thoughtful observer should be wary of making clear cut distinctions not only between good taste and bad but also between the symbolic logic that generates a design by Thomas Jefferson and the common sense that shapes the design of a storefront. For example, it is possible to perceive a particular motif presented in Palladio's Four Books of Architecture spread beyond the confines of Jefferson's personal library into the realm of pattern books published "for the trade." In this process the motif breaks free of the bonds of "good taste" that claim to circumscribe its "proper" context and define its "correct" meaning. In referring to the motif the designer of a storefront is not referring to the validity of Palladio's formulation but rather to its formal solidity as a cultural symbol for reasons not much different than Jefferson's. Implicit in the work of both designers there is an assertion of the necessity for an American architecture rooted in popular consciousness that has the same imperative quality as Palladio's reworking of Roman architectural motifs for Venice in a period of transformation.

AIRPORT SHUTTLE. In the closing decades of the 20th century the city of the plains has evolved into a clustered constellation in a permanent state of transformation. In the early 19th century the city was entered from the river, later from the surrounding countryside. Today an ever increasing number of people, services, and goods jet down to the airstrips of an inter-

162

national airport; an adjacent corporate center of office buildings, hotels, and conference facilities; and a developing cargo-industrial complex. This cluster is linked with others by an interconnected grid of communication networks and high-speed, multi-lane highways. Unfortunately, the particular cluster that developed to the north of the Main Street I've been discussing seems to have been the result of economic calculations and growth projections that have fallen short, for there is little to see on the drive here from the central city or one of its older suburbs than links of a highway system and too many signs announcing "space available." Nevertheless, the reorientation of the underlying grid to air travel has already had an irreversible impact on the lives of everyone who lives or works within driving distance of these under-used facilities. For example, the menu of a restaurant that used to advertise itself as the best "steak house" in the region now features "fresh fish flown in daily."

Even the abundance of available development sites has an impact, for it tends to reduce land costs and encourage the construction of land-extensive manufacturing arrangements. There is a general movement of manufacturing away from the central city and older suburbs towards this developing network of global communication and transportation facilities. This outward movement entails decentralization of employment opportunities as well as expansion of municipal services, such as sewage treatment and disposal; utilities, such as water and electricity; and household conveniences, such as remote television reception via satellite dishes. There is a general tendency to favor new locations over old ones, new construction over rehabilitation or reuse of existing facilities, private means of transportation over public transit, owner-occupied houses over multiple-family rental units.

All of this confounds any theory of urban development that assumes a monocentric city with a growing population and defies any theory of urban design associated with classicism, new-urbanism, or any other -ism. The published summary of a study organized by a school of architecture located on the Atlantic seaboard is both representative and revealing. Some of the essays in the publication were developed from contributions to the school's lecture series, others from work done in its studio and seminar courses, and the remainder were solicited from professional colleagues in the region. All of the essays share a common concern:

They challenge the suburban paradigm that has swept our nation in the form of look-alike subdivisions, spot development of commercial areas, and office parks sprouting along our highways... [The essays] also point to the fact that the same paradigm which has controlled suburban form has been destructive of the [central] city as well, eroding its fabric, cutting it into pieces, and isolating its remnant areas from one another... [The authors observe] a loss of centeredness offered by traditional towns or cities which encourage social assembly on both an informal and formal basis.

In short, the authors identify the paradigm of the dispersed city of the plains as the bad guy and associate the good guy with "ideal planning principles" which can be traced back to

plans based on Roman classical town planning principles... on the Gothic city, Renaissance city, the Arts and Crafts Movement [of England in the late 19th century], the Bauhaus... towns and villages [that] are far-ranging, mixed-use communities carefully balanced to minimize the need for residents to travel off-site to meet daily needs... [and] planned so that most residences are located within a short walk of a central urban square as well as a surrounding greenbelt [for example, the English New Towns Movement of the mid-20th century]...

Another group of essays based on rejection of "the paradigmatic qualities of fragmentation," this time appearing in an English architectural magazine, peers towards the future rather than the past:

...the once binary metropolis [that is, center/edge opposition] has exploded into a regional carpet of autonomous communities... The concept of speed and fragment does not restrict itself solely to the effect of the car [and air travel]. Through the accelerating development of regional and global communication networks... time is compressed to such an extent that we can no longer build up an image [such as "Gothic city" or "Renaissance city"] of what a city should be...

Yet the first essay concludes with the image of "a city represented by an architecture that is less and less materia, an architecture that is primarily process and secondarily fragments"-- in other words, an image of the city

of the plains. Unfortunately, none of the essays and projects that follow develop this image. Quite the opposite, this image suggests to one commentator a "broken kaleidoscope" in which architectural elements "fail to coalesce" into recognizable patterns; each fragment appears isolated, wholly internalized. Another essayist suggests that such an image and the communal image that every "true city" requires are mutually exclusive. All seem to agree:

The challenge is to impose effective boundaries and limits to growth on [the built form of the

166

American city] whose very nature, Frank Lloyd Wright recognized, is to be everywhere or nowhere; to create or to redevelop genuine cores for a decentralized city that has grown by ignoring centers; to provide alternatives for the automobile...

In short, "in a quest for [so-called] new strategies for the 21st century," old utopian images are called up. There are repeated references to modernist utopias such as Ebenezer Howard's Garden City (1900s), the Soviet De-urbanist City (1920s), or Le Corbusier's Radiant City and Wright's Broadacre City (1930s). However, there is no effort made to confront the more recent postmodern rejection of this line of planning and architectural theory, nor to explain their own rejection of "the paradigmatic qualities of urban fragmentation."

Both groups of essayists and designers seem to share a horror fragmenti. They argue that the built form of the dispersed city is poorly articulated and inadequately elaborated. It is not only fragmentary but repetitive and tangled up into indecipherable, discontinuous patterns that are everywhere but lead urban design nowhere. I am tempted to reply: "How right you are!" and leave it at that. However,

their horror fragmenti with all of its theoretical assumptions and pretentious "quest for ambitious new forms of urbanity" demands attention.

The architectural fragments of the dispersed city have only recently broken free from the design restrictions of the walled cities of Europe and its American colonies. The built form of the city of the plains has been in the making only over the last 100, at most 150 years. In a word, the results are inconclusive. It would seem that analysis of a built form that is still poorly articulated and inadequately elaborated calls for a few methodological precautions. In the first place, the analysis need not concern itself with regulated and historically legitimated central city configurations; with the architectural mechanisms through which they are made manifest, such as articulation of "the heart" of the city; nor with the social effects of these, such as the custom of promenading "along the avenue" on Easter Sunday. On the contrary, the analysis should be concerned with architecture where it becomes capillary, where it distances itself from both historical precedents and science-fiction projections -- which is to say, where it is invested in mundane and effective tasks.

168

To give an example, a proposal presented in the English magazine is intended "to counter sprawl at the periphery" of Dallas - Fort Worth, Texas:

On the fringe of the modern city, displaced fragments sprout without intrinsic relationships to existing organization other than the camber and loops of the curvilinear freeway...This zone calls for visions and projections to delineate the boundary between the urban and the rural...

Spiroid Sectors: Future residents are transported to new town sectors by a high-speed MAGLEV transit from the Dallas-Fort Worth Airport. A new hierarchy of public spaces is surrounded by... coiling armatures [that] contain a hybrid of macro-programmes... The smallest spiroids form low-cost [sic] courtyard housing in experimental thin/thick wall construction.

I believe that the analysis called for is the exact opposite of this architectural fairy tale and any design proposal in which the built environment is reduced to a distillation of whimsical "visions and projections." Insofar as this particular distillation represents an urban "sector," it is an amalgamation of "public transit stations, health clubs, cinemas, galleries [and] domestic activities... knotted in a continuous space-forming morphology." Well, rather than wor-

(after HOLL)

169

ry about fragments sprouting on the fringe of Dallas-Fort Worth without intrinsic relationships to existing organization, the author of this proposal, Steven Holl, might have tried to examine how built forms are constituted as peripheral fragments as a result of the effects of that organization. I suspect that the existing organization is something that circulates, something that functions in the form of a constellation. Not only do the architectural fragments circulate among its treads, they are always in the position of simultaneously being shaped by and shaping the web-like structure. They are both causes and effects.

The "spiroid sector" of Holl's proposal may be identified and examined as an "urban district," a less glamorous but more accessible term. As such, it should not be perceived as a sort of nucleus, an inert mass of building material to which people are transported and in which they are subdued and crushed as individuals, as Holl does in graphic as well as verbal terms. Rather, the architectural observer should focus on the mechanisms of the organization, the circulation of architectural fragments. Each of these fragments has its own historical trajectory; each has been transformed, displaced, extended by regional, national, and international design currents. These currents can be identified and, I believe, the manner in which they have engaged with each architectural fragment, each building technology of the urban constellation that is called Dallas-Fort Worth, can be revealed.

By way of summarizing, I would say that

urban students, planners, and designers in the United States must eschew the centralizing model of the European and early American city, which has played out its historical roles. First, it was a mechanism of control that was effective in the formation of trade centers and city-states, such as Venice in the late Middle Ages and Florence in the Renaissance. Then, it served as the major instrument in bringing an aristocracy under the control of royal power, such as the Paris of Louis XIII and Versailles of Louis XIV. In the 18th century, it functioned in opposition to administrative monarchy -- London is a good example, as is a rebellious colonial outpost, such as Boston. In the latter half of the 19th century, the emergence or rather invention of the dispersed city of the plains represented a new mechanism of control that, I believe, has proven to be incompatible with the old centralized urban model. Enough time has elapsed, enough evidence has been produced, to begin developing new theories of city planning and urban design.

SOURCES

Eco, Umberto. The Open Work. Cambridge: Harvard University Press, 1989.

Elazar, Daniel. Cities of the Prairie. New York: Basic Books, 1970.

Erlich, George. Kansas City, Missouri: An Architectural History. Kansas City: Historic Kansas City Foundation, 1979.

Foucault, Michel. "Two Lectures," Power/Knowledge: Selected Interviews and Other Writings, 1972-1977. New York: Pantheon Books, 1980.

Grant, H. Roger. Kansas Depots. Topeka: Kansas State Historical Society, 1990.

Hurt, S. and Thadani, D. (editors). Making Towns. College Park, Maryland: School of Architecture, University of Maryland, 1994.

Larsen, Lawrence. The Urban West at the End of the Frontier. Lawrence: The Regents Press of Kansas, 1978.

Mahoney, Timothy. River Towns in the Great West. Cambridge: Cambridge University Press, 1990.

Pierson, William. The Colonial and Neoclassical Styles. New York: Doubleday, 1970.

Toy, M. (editor). "The Periphery." Architectural Design Magazine. Profile No. 108, March-April, 1994.

Leer las terceras críticas como un
trabajo de escritura liberal -

— El —

— en lo sublime — un contexto —
el valor de lo bello —
la cantidad — intensidad

Gracián como el antes —
reboroma — El Arte de agudezas
— un lenguaje de competir —
ofensivo y defensivo —
la retórica — y su lenguaje —
— un corte — la retórica — la
dialéctica —

Cada refleja un ser/juego que
responde a sus intereses —
— una estética — el ...
una moral — los ...

(Cuál es el valor de la belleza.
es de la cultura y cual fund
la libertad a la polit. es.)
_____

- el valor de la belleza -
- Idelogia - politica - filosofica -
- el valor de la libertad -
independiente de cualquier norma
de valoración -
El contexto de la belleza - la belleza como
resultado - no ~~algo~~ como proceso
sus historia - supuestos - del
- todo lo cual se pue pretender -
- el gusto - es a la cultura - lo fu
el individuo a la politica -
- el sentido de lo bello -
- la obra de arte en la epoca de la
- reproduccion industrial -
- Marx a Benjamin -
- la universalidad - de lo bello -